FOOD AND DRINK · FOR VEGAN LOVERS ·

RECIPES

Belong to

....

....

....

The Food and Drink Recipes for Vegan Lovers is one of the eight cookbooks published as part of a larger collection designed to help you write your own recipes in one place and have them at hand when you cook your favorite meals.

This **Special Collection** also includes:

- **SOUPS**
- **SALADS**
- **PASTRIES**
- **APPETIZERS**
- **DIET RECIPES**
- **OVEN RECIPES**
- **CAKES AND PIES**

Table of Contents

Recipe	Page

# Table of Contents

Recipe	Page

# Table of Contents

Recipe	Page

 # Table of Contents 

Recipe	Page

Table of Contents

Recipe	Page

Recipe: _______________________________ 

Prep time: ______   **Cook time:** ______   **Servings:** ______

Ingredients

Directions

Notes

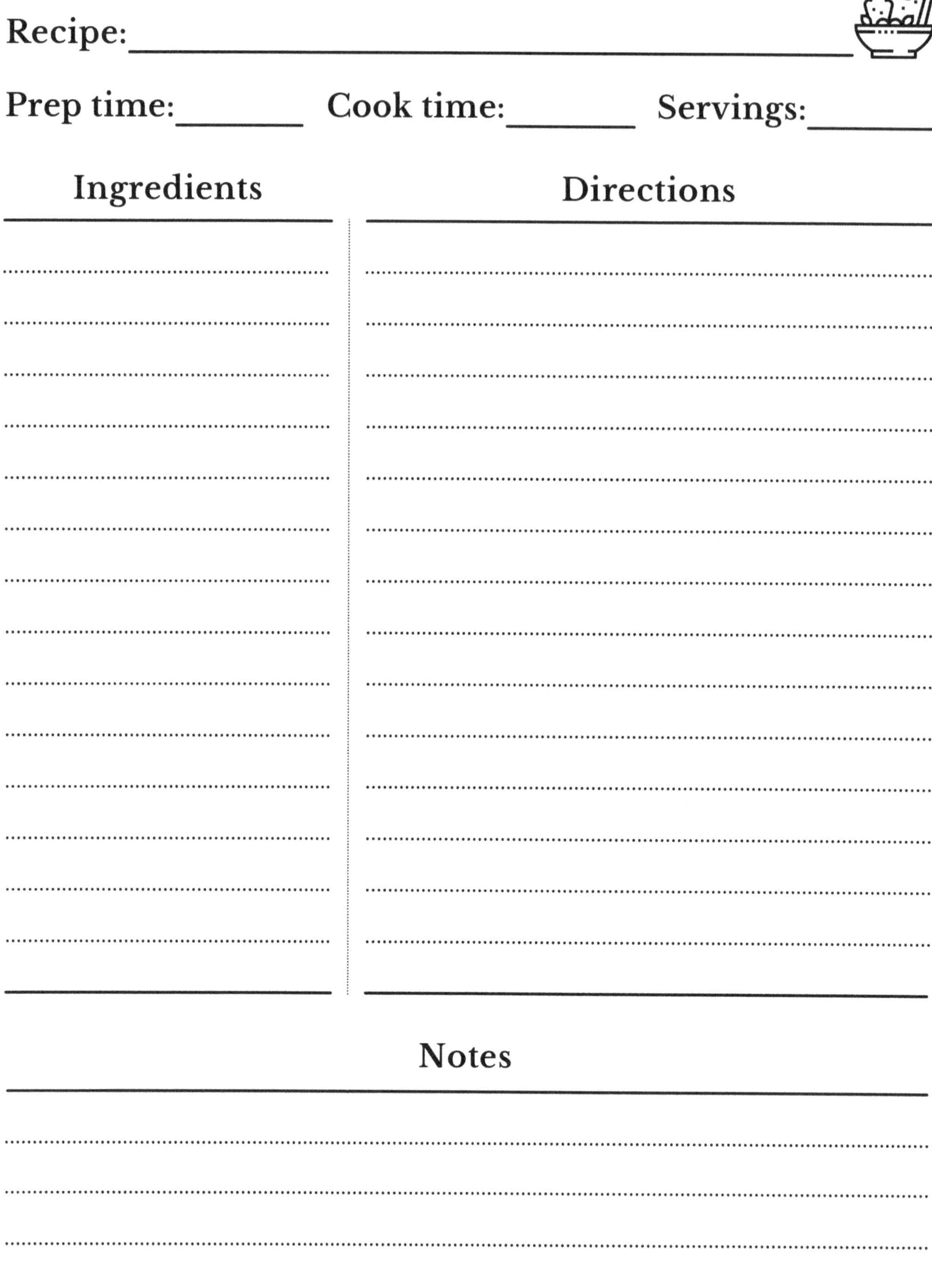

Recipe:____

Prep time:________   Cook time:________   Servings:________

Ingredients

Directions

Notes

Recipe:_______________________

Prep time:________   Cook time:________   Servings:________

Ingredients

Directions

Notes

Recipe:_______________________________________

Prep time:_______   Cook time:________   Servings:________

Ingredients

Directions

Notes

Recipe:

Prep time: _______ Cook time: _______ Servings: _______

Ingredients

Directions

Notes

Recipe:

Prep time:______ Cook time:______ Servings:______

Ingredients

Directions

Notes

Recipe: _______________________________________ 

Prep time: _______   Cook time: _______   Servings: _______

Ingredients

Directions

Notes

Recipe:

Prep time: _______ **Cook time:** _______ **Servings:** _______

Ingredients

Directions

Notes

Recipe:_______________________________________ 

Prep time:________   Cook time:________   Servings:________

| Ingredients | Directions |

Notes

Recipe:

Prep time:＿＿＿＿＿ Cook time:＿＿＿＿＿ Servings:＿＿＿＿＿

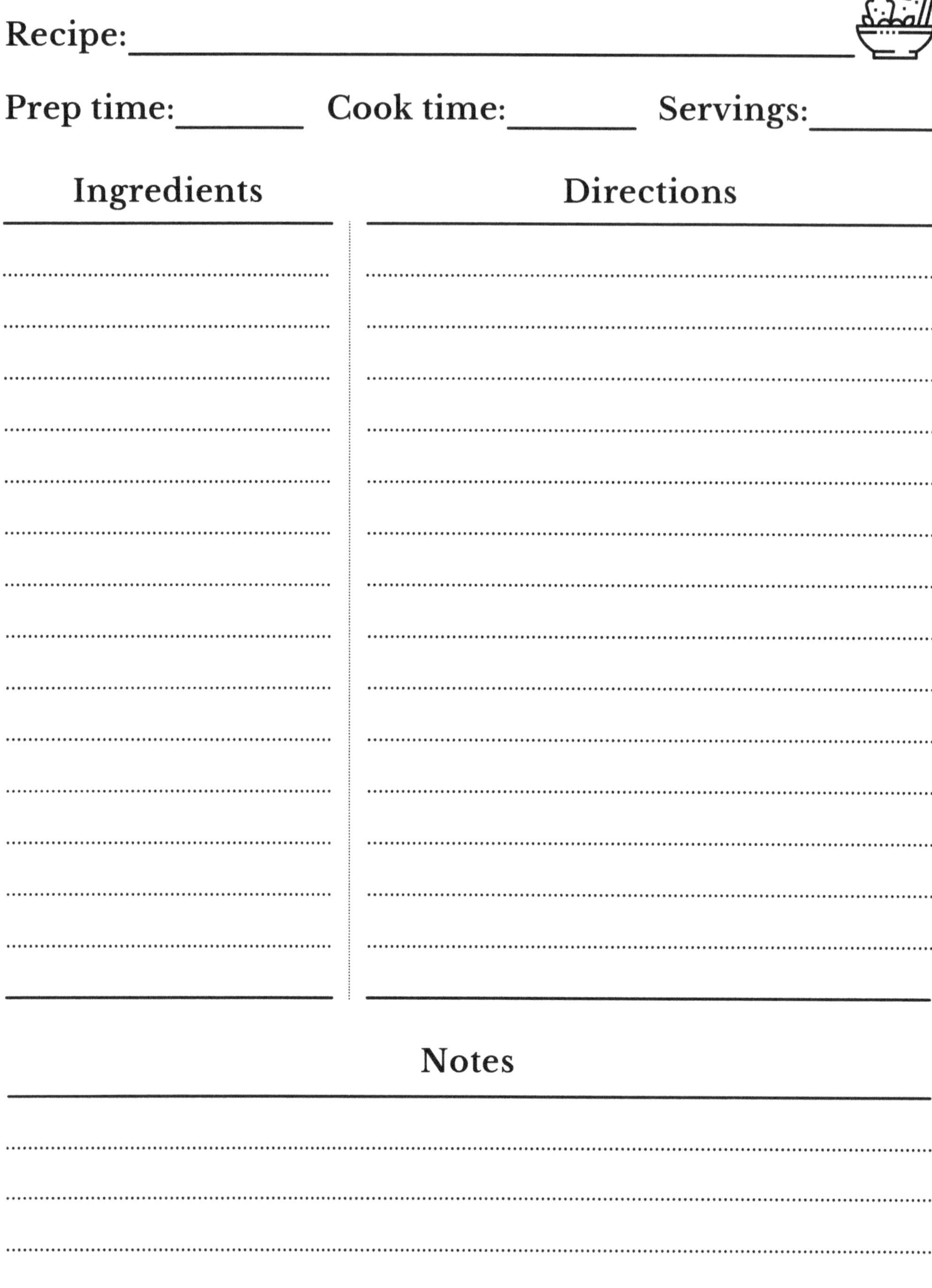

Ingredients

Directions

Notes

Recipe:_______________________________________

Prep time:________   Cook time:________   Servings:________

Ingredients

Directions

Notes

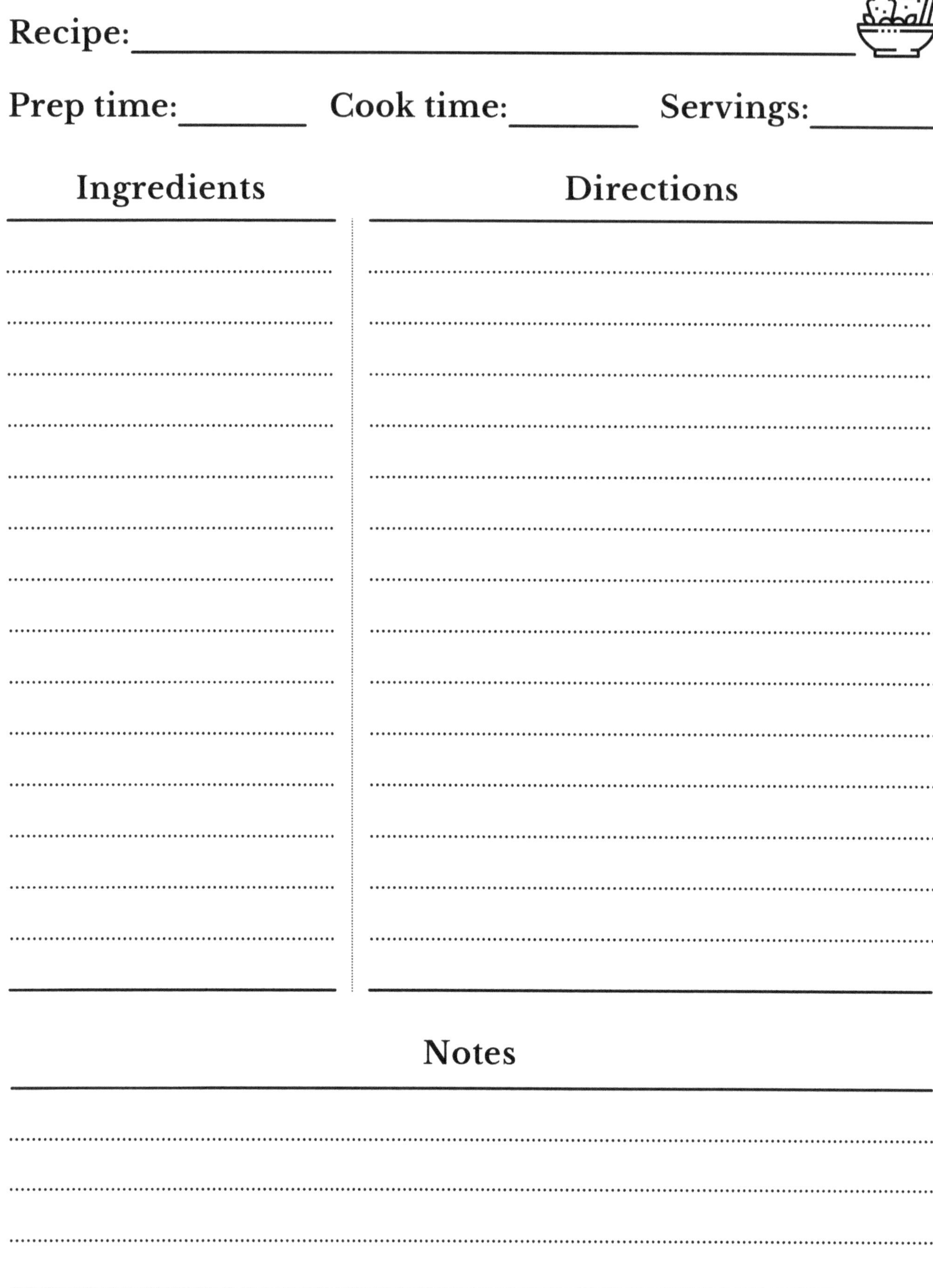

Recipe:____

Prep time:________   Cook time:________   Servings:________

Ingredients

Directions

Notes

Recipe:_______________________________________ 

Prep time:_______   Cook time:_______   Servings:_______

Ingredients

Directions

Notes

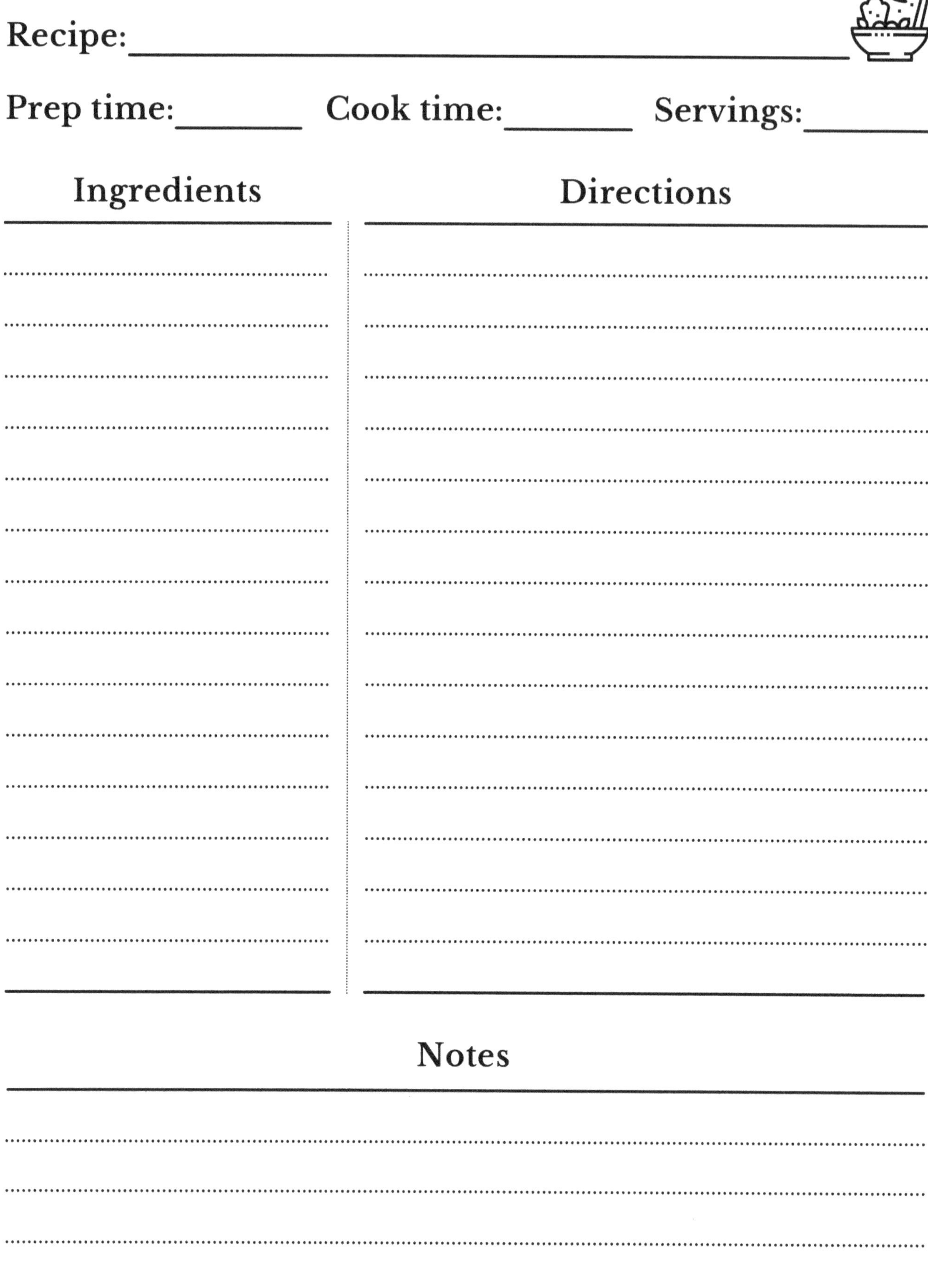

Recipe:____

Prep time:________   Cook time:________   Servings:________

Ingredients	Directions

Notes

Recipe:_______________________________

Prep time:_______ **Cook time:**_______ **Servings:**_______

Ingredients

Directions

Notes

Recipe:_______________________________________

Prep time:________   Cook time:________   Servings:________

Ingredients

Directions

Notes

Recipe:_______________________

Prep time:_______ **Cook time:**_______ **Servings:**_______

Ingredients

Directions

Notes

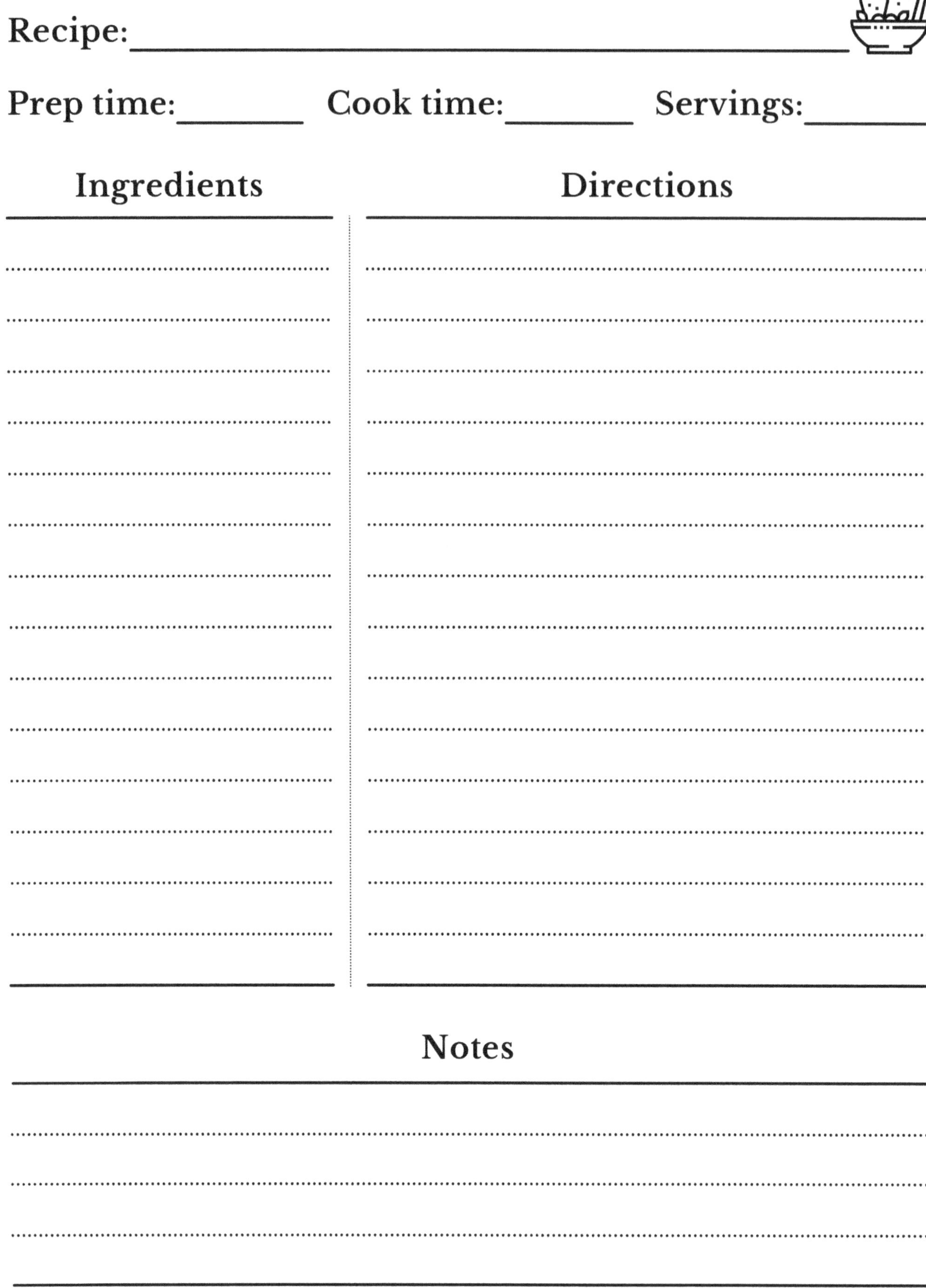

Recipe:_______________________________________

Prep time:________   Cook time:________   Servings:________

Ingredients

Directions

Notes

Recipe: _______________________________

Prep time: ______ Cook time: ______ Servings: ______

Ingredients	Directions

Notes

Recipe:___________________________ 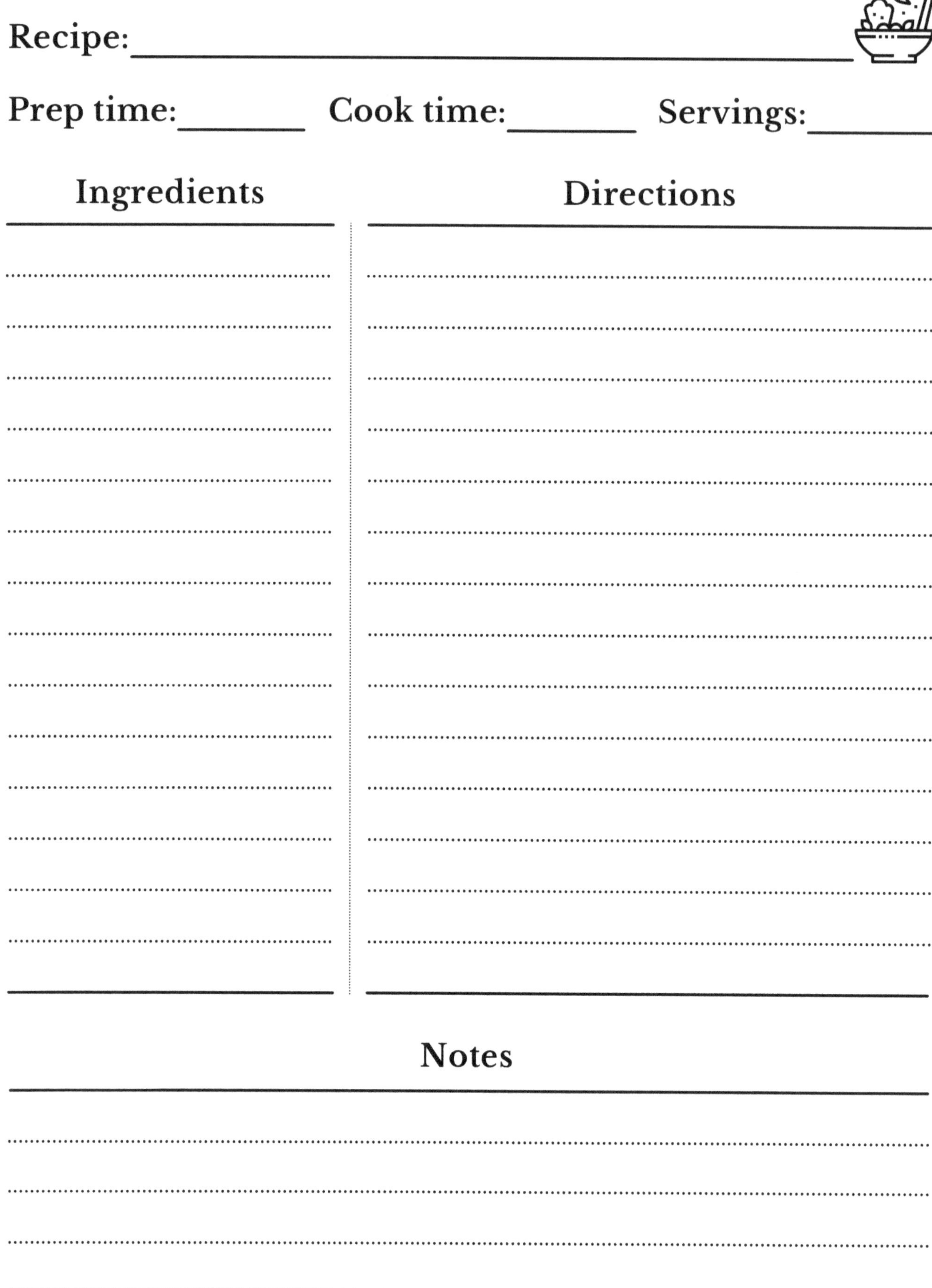

Prep time:_______ Cook time:_______ Servings:_______

Ingredients

Directions

Notes

Recipe:_______________________________________ 

Prep time:________   Cook time:________   Servings:________

Ingredients

Directions

Notes

Recipe:____ 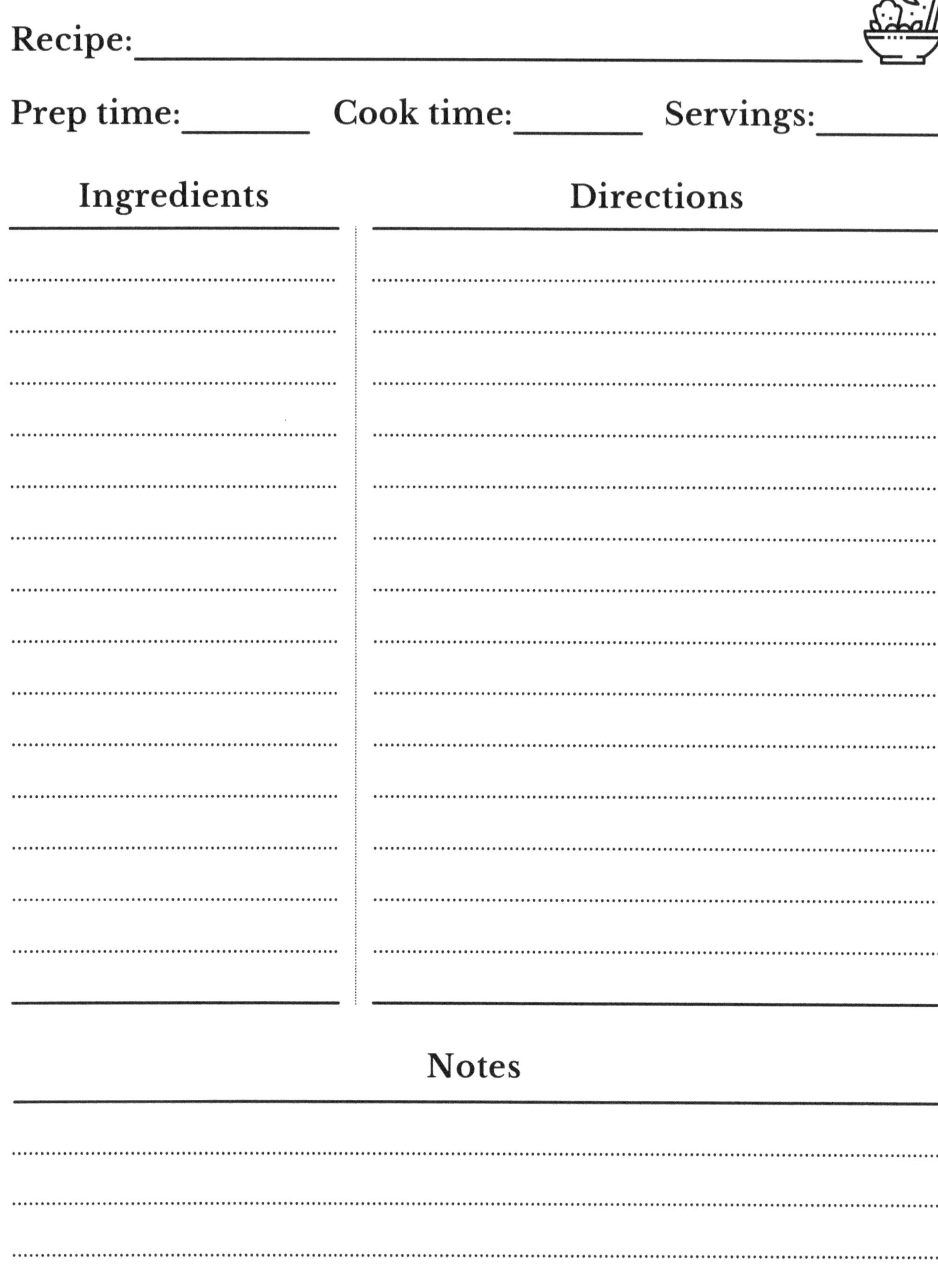

Prep time:________   Cook time:________   Servings:________

Ingredients	Directions

Notes

Recipe:____ 

Prep time:________   Cook time:________   Servings:________

Ingredients

Directions

Notes

Recipe:_________________________________ 

Prep time:________   Cook time:________   Servings:________

Ingredients	Directions

Notes

Recipe:____ 

Prep time:________   Cook time:________   Servings:________

Ingredients

Directions

Notes

Recipe:

Prep time: ______ **Cook time:** ______ **Servings:** ______

Ingredients

Directions

Notes

Recipe:_______________________________ 

Prep time:______ **Cook time:**______ **Servings:**______

Ingredients

Directions

Notes

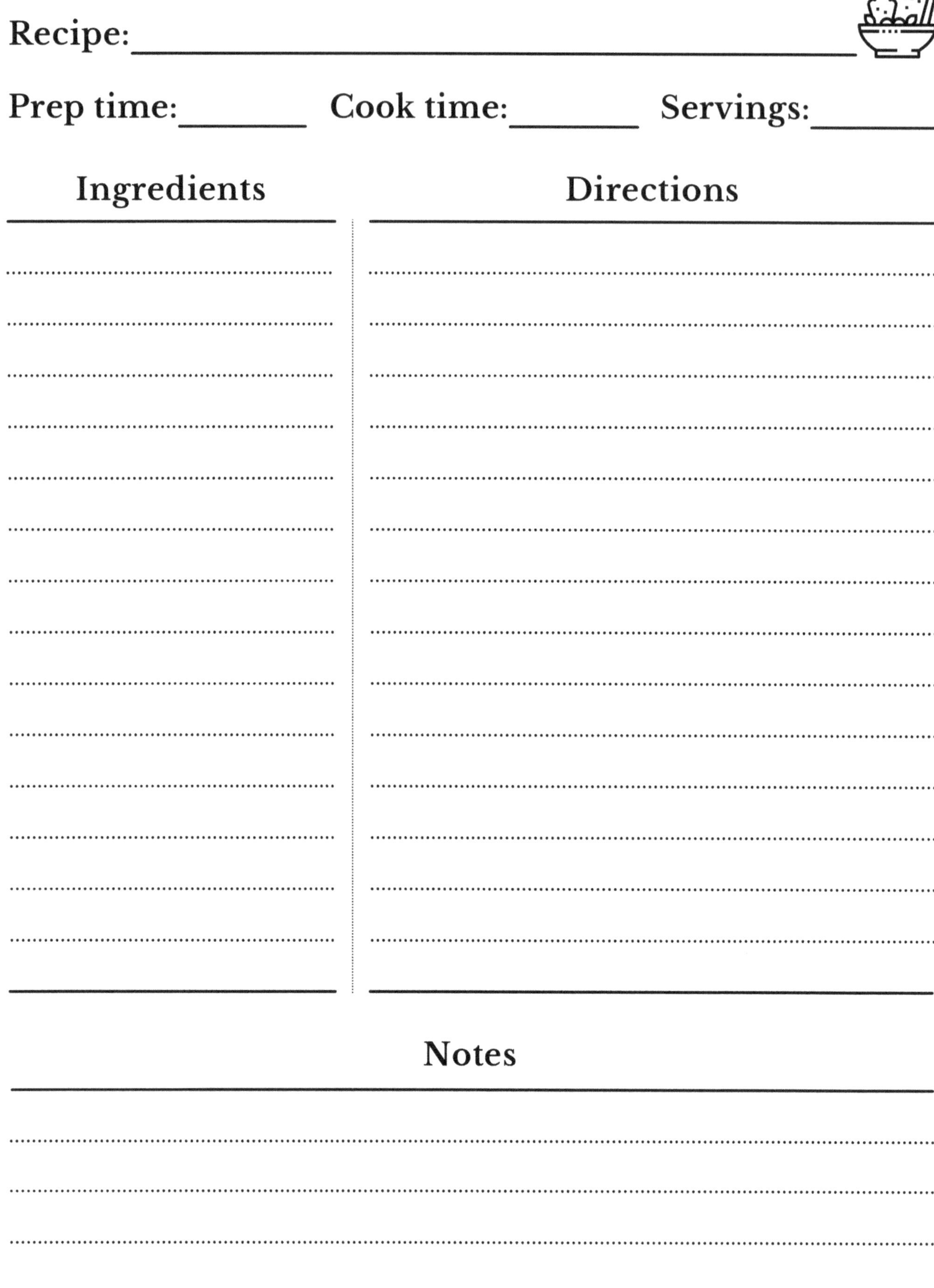

Recipe:

Prep time: _______ **Cook time:** _______ **Servings:** _______

Ingredients

Directions

Notes

Recipe:____ 

Prep time:_______   **Cook time:**_______   **Servings:**_______

Ingredients

Directions

Notes

Recipe:____ 

Prep time:_______ **Cook time:**_______ **Servings:**_______

Ingredients	Directions

Notes

Recipe:___________________________________ 

Prep time:_______ **Cook time:**_______ **Servings:**_______

Ingredients

Directions

Notes

Recipe:__________________________________

Prep time:________   Cook time:________   Servings:________

Ingredients

Directions

Notes

Recipe:________________________________ 

Prep time:_______ Cook time:_______ Servings:_______

Ingredients

Directions

Notes

Recipe:_______________________________________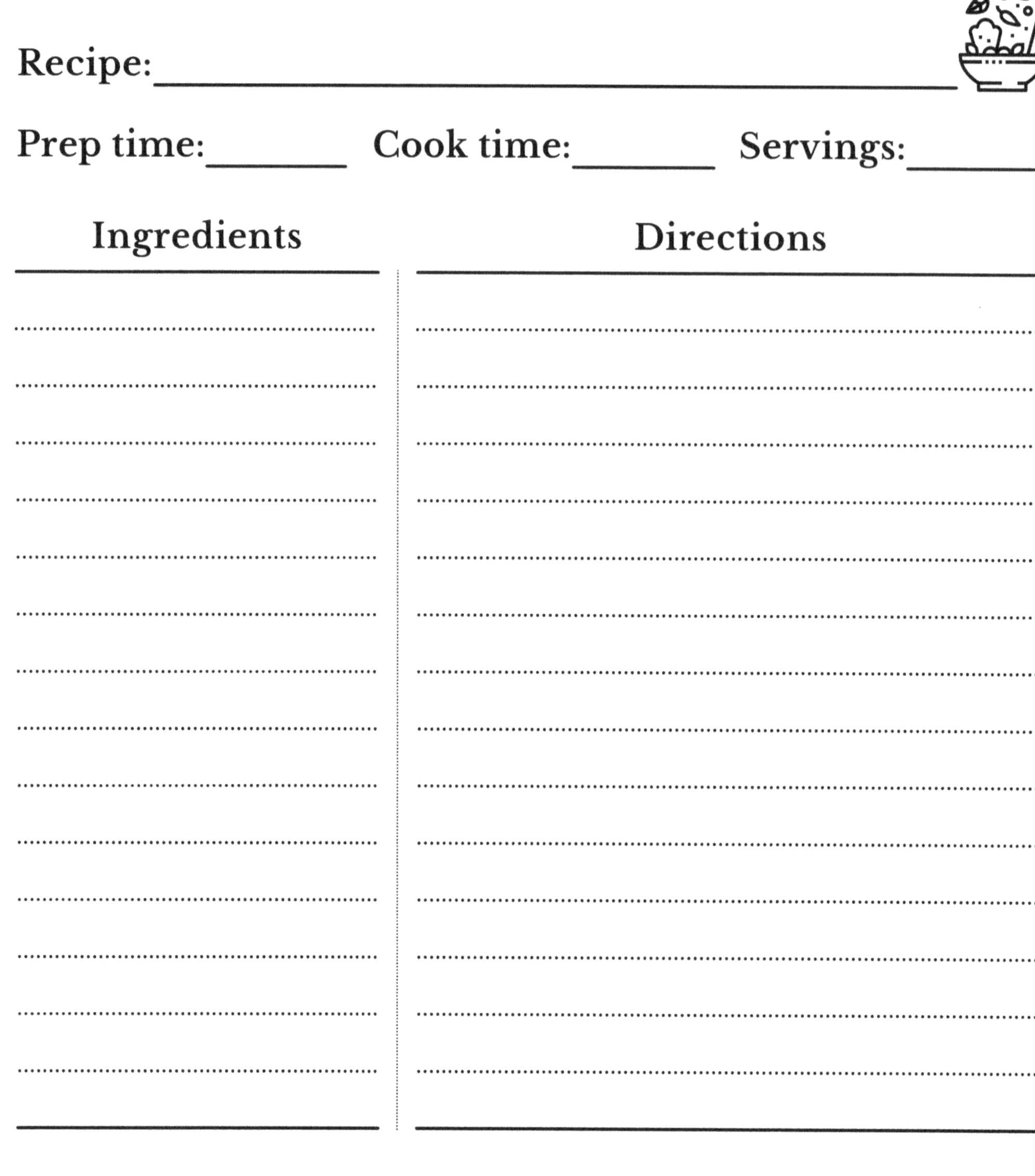

Prep time:________   Cook time:________   Servings:________

Ingredients

Directions

Notes

Recipe:_______________________________________ 

Prep time:________   Cook time:________   Servings:________

Ingredients

Directions

Notes

Recipe:____

Prep time:________   Cook time:________   Servings:________

Ingredients

Directions

Notes

Recipe:_______________________________ 

Prep time:_______   Cook time:_______   Servings:_______

Ingredients

Directions

Notes

Recipe:_______________________________________

Prep time:_______ Cook time:_______ Servings:_______

Ingredients

Directions

Notes

Recipe:_______________________________________ 

Prep time:________   Cook time:________   Servings:________

Ingredients

Directions

Notes

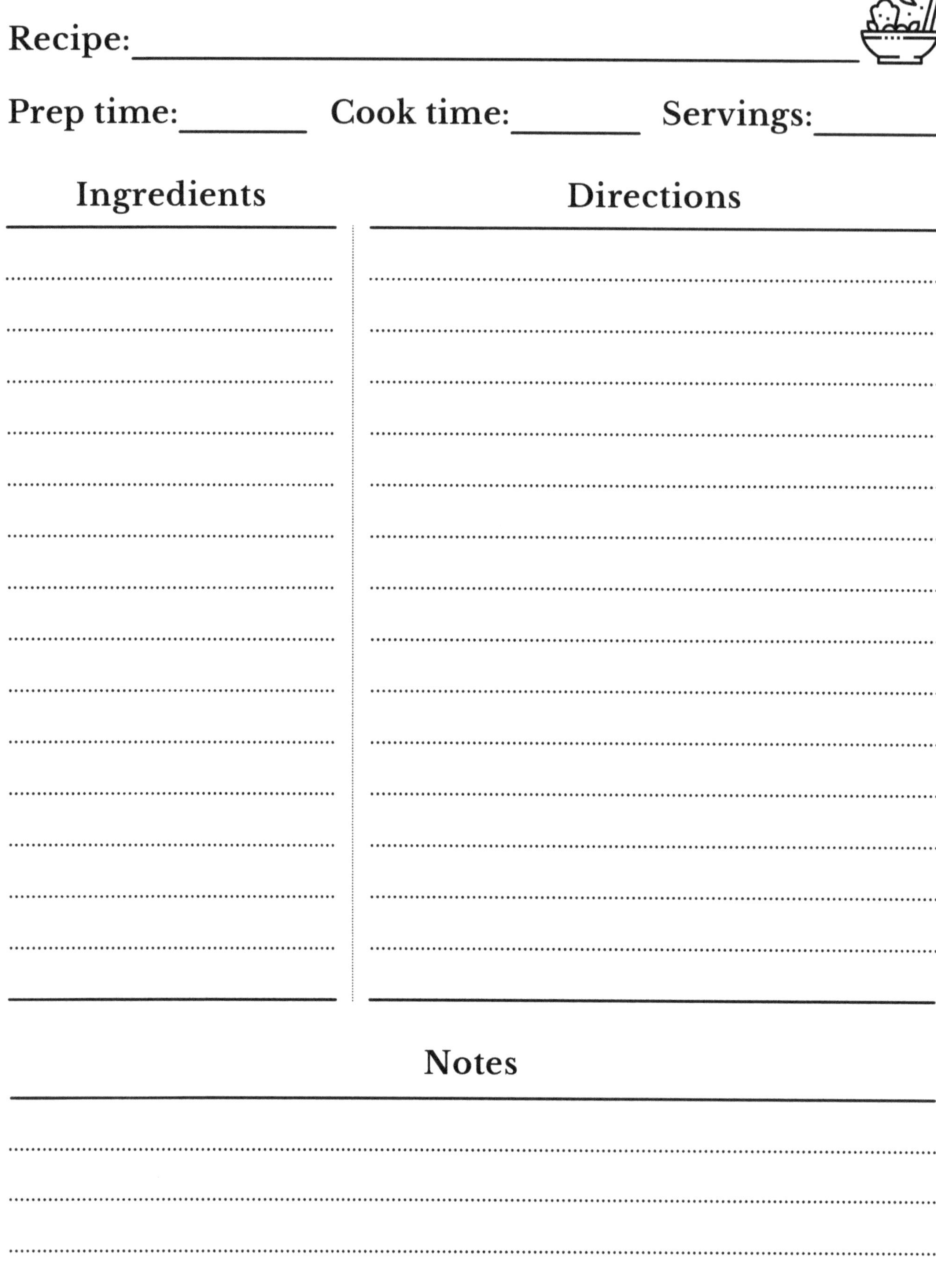

Recipe:

Prep time: ______ **Cook time:** ______ **Servings:** ______

Ingredients

Directions

Notes

Recipe:

Prep time: _______   Cook time: _______   Servings: _______

Ingredients

Directions

Notes

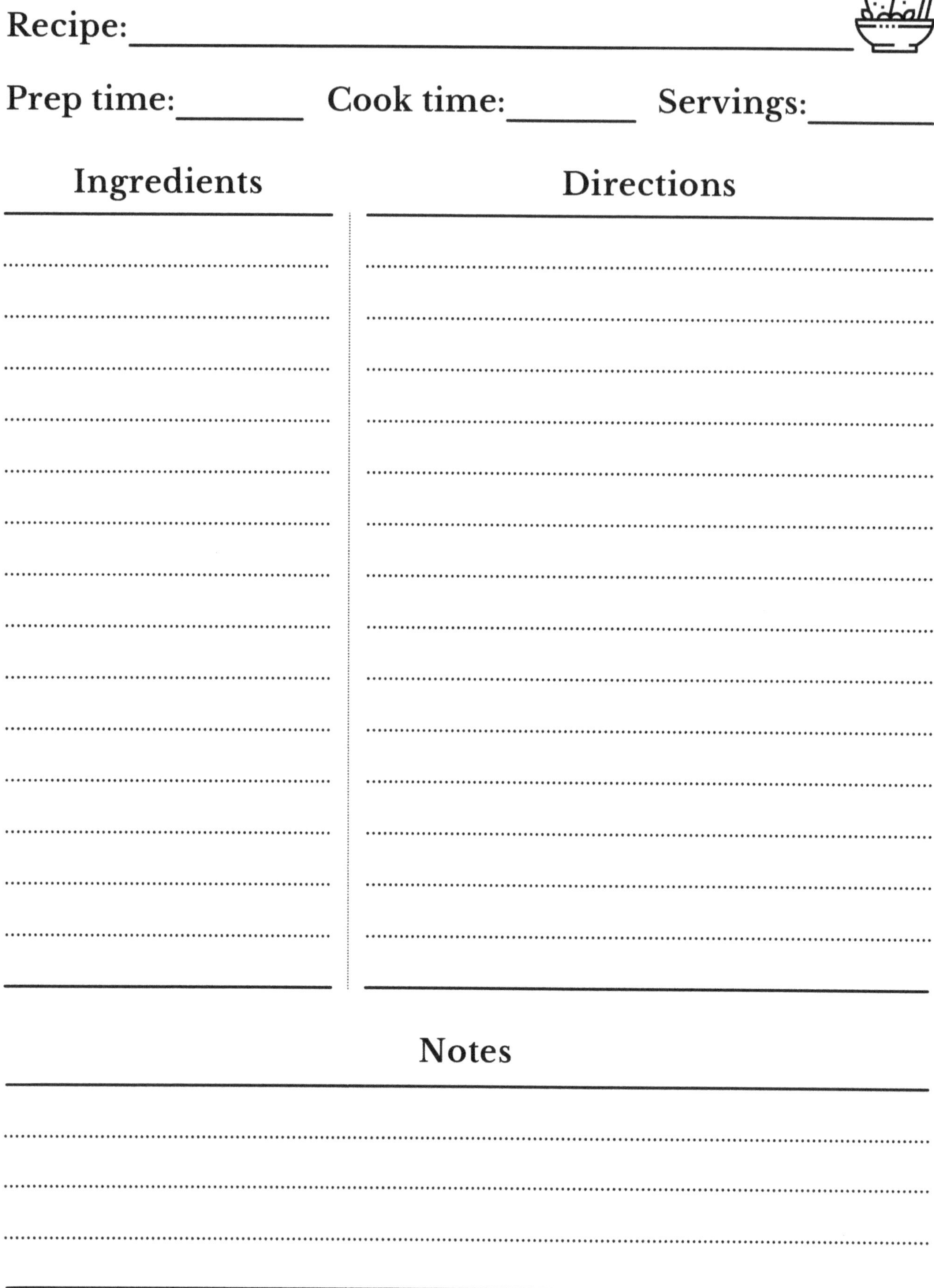

Recipe:

Prep time: _______ **Cook time:** _______ **Servings:** _______

Ingredients

Directions

Notes

Recipe:_______________________________________ 

Prep time:________ Cook time:________ Servings:________

Ingredients

Directions

Notes

Recipe:____

Prep time:_______   Cook time:_______   Servings:_______

| Ingredients | Directions |

Notes

Recipe:________________________________ 

Prep time:______   Cook time:______   Servings:______

Ingredients

Directions

Notes

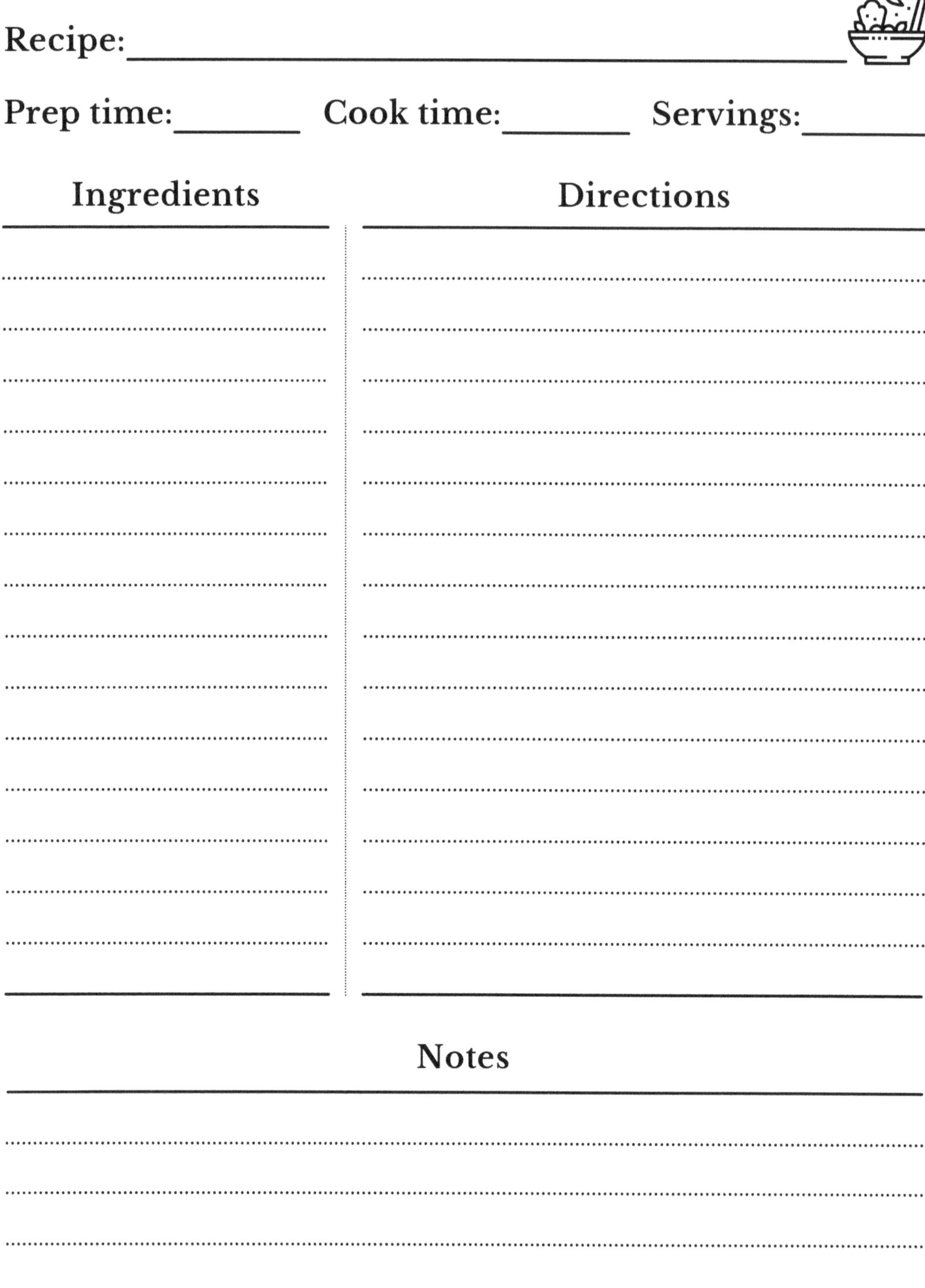

Recipe:____

Prep time:________ **Cook time:**________ **Servings:**________

Ingredients

Directions

Notes

Recipe:____ 

Prep time:________   Cook time:________   Servings:________

Ingredients

Directions

Notes

Recipe:_______________________________________

Prep time:_______ Cook time:_______ Servings:_______

Ingredients

Directions

Notes

Recipe:_______________________________________ 

Prep time:_______   Cook time:_______   Servings:_______

Ingredients

Directions

Notes

Recipe:____

Prep time:_______   Cook time:_______   Servings:_______

Ingredients

Directions

Notes

Recipe:

Prep time:_______ Cook time:_______ Servings:_______

Ingredients

Directions

Notes

Recipe:____

Prep time:________   Cook time:________   Servings:________

Ingredients

Directions

Notes

Recipe:____ 

Prep time:_______   Cook time:_______   Servings:_______

Ingredients

Directions

Notes

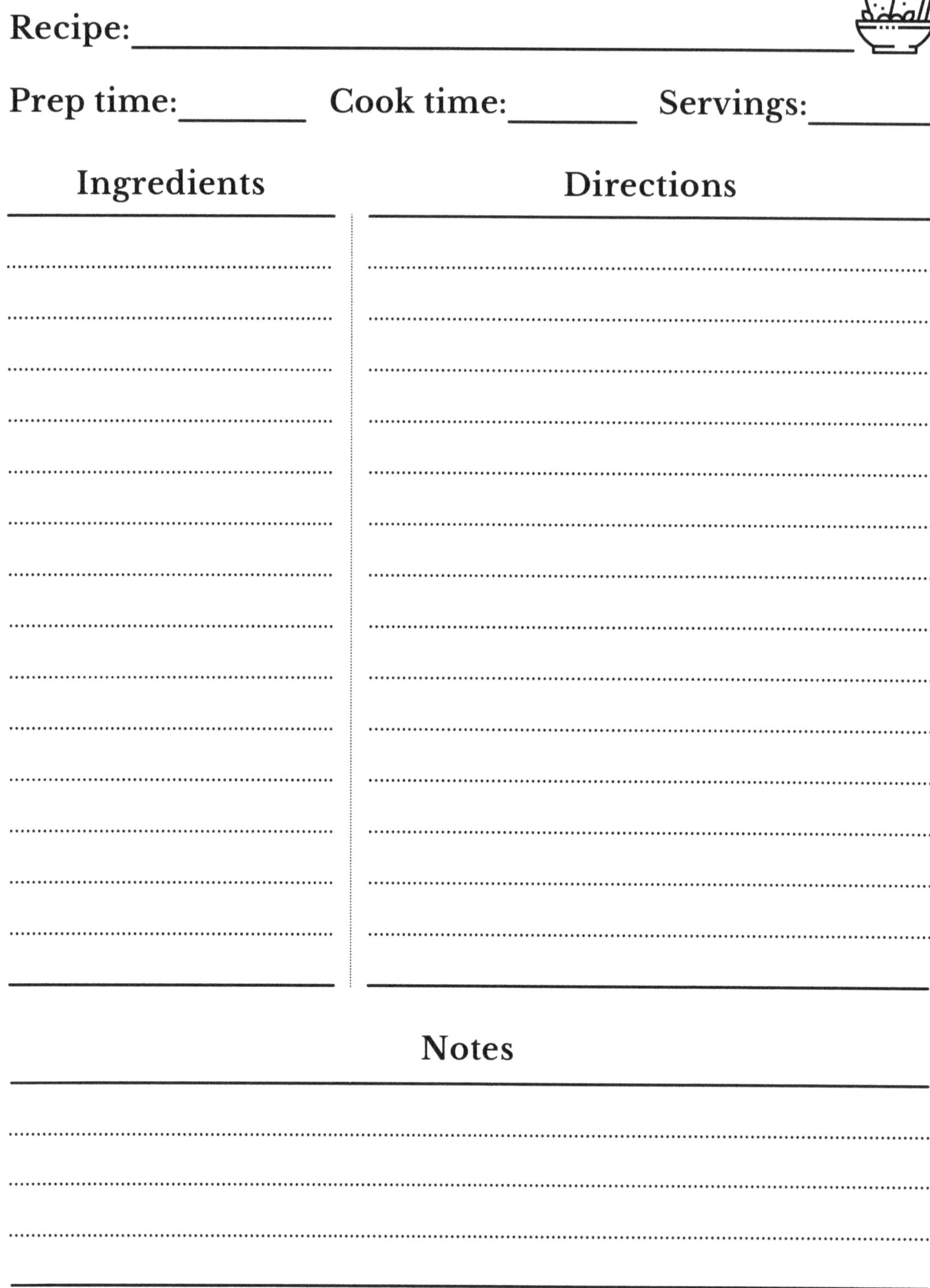

Recipe:____

Prep time:________   Cook time:________   Servings:________

Ingredients

Directions

Notes

Recipe:____ 

Prep time:_______   Cook time:_______   Servings:_______

Ingredients

Directions

Notes

Recipe: ____

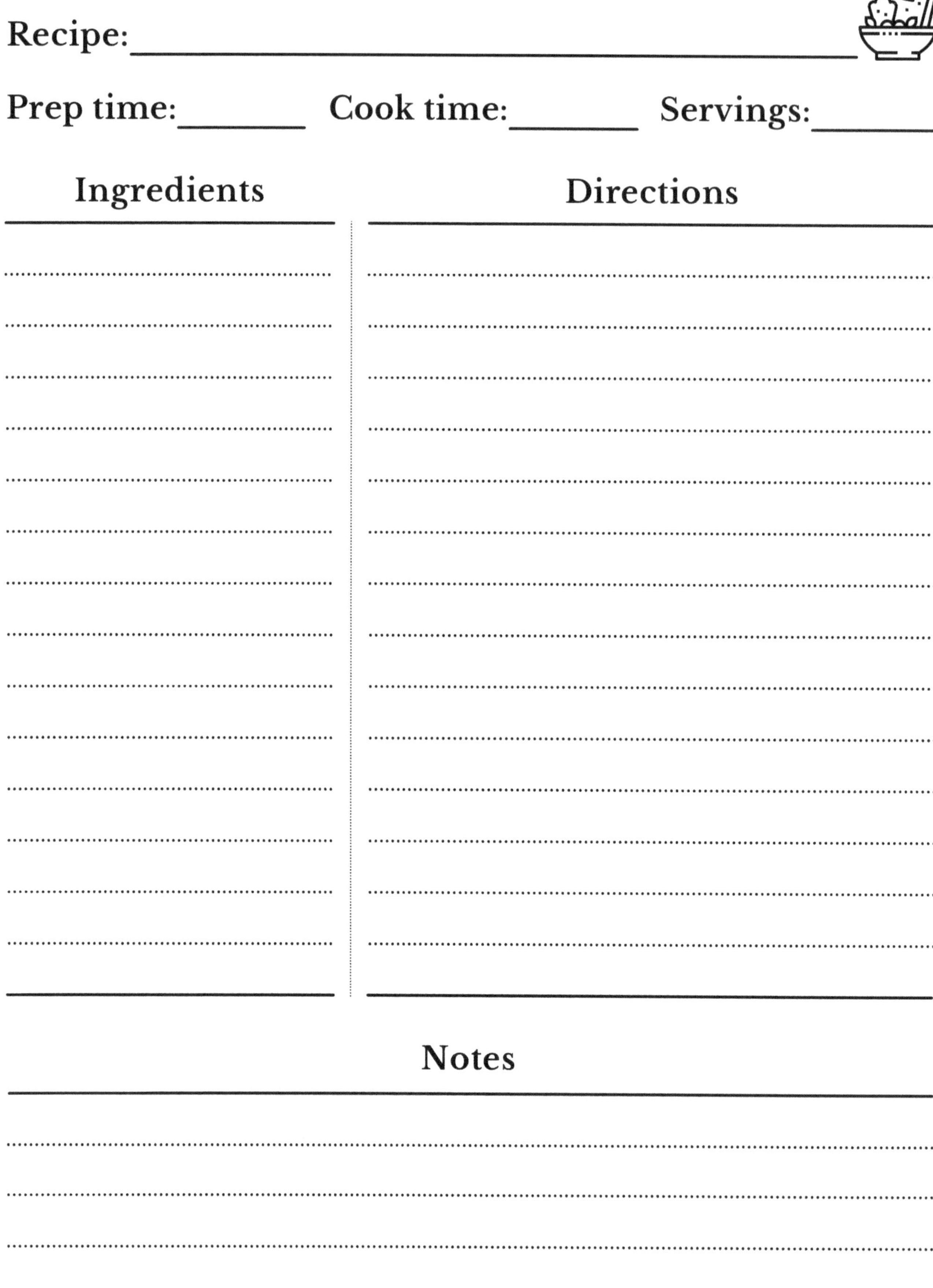

Prep time: _______   **Cook time:** _______   **Servings:** _______

Ingredients

Directions

Notes

Recipe:_______________________________________ 

Prep time:_______   Cook time:_______   Servings:_______

Ingredients	Directions

Notes

Recipe:_______________________________________ 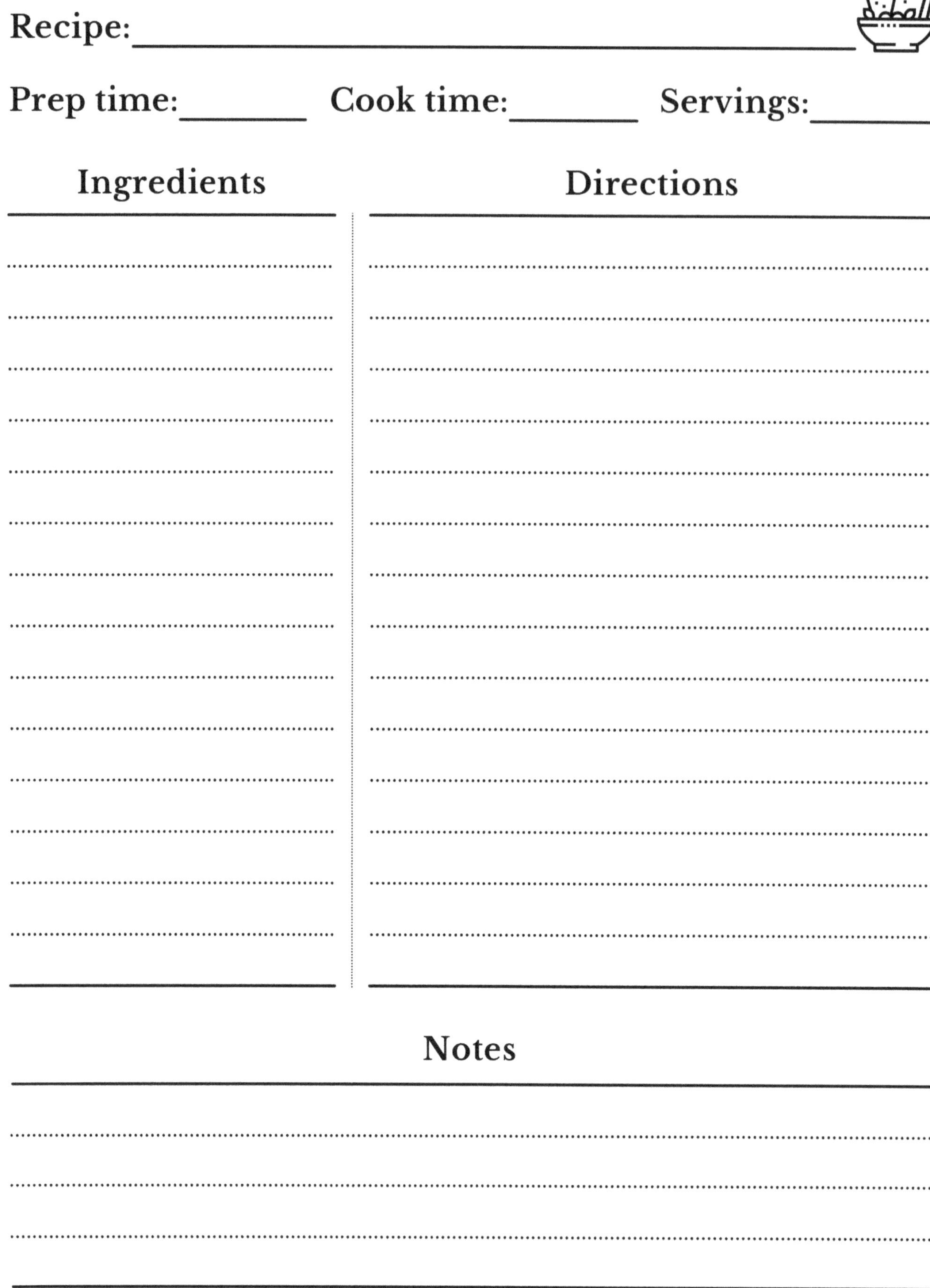

Prep time:________   Cook time:________   Servings:________

Ingredients

Directions

Notes

Recipe:____

Prep time:________ Cook time:________ Servings:________

Ingredients	Directions

Notes

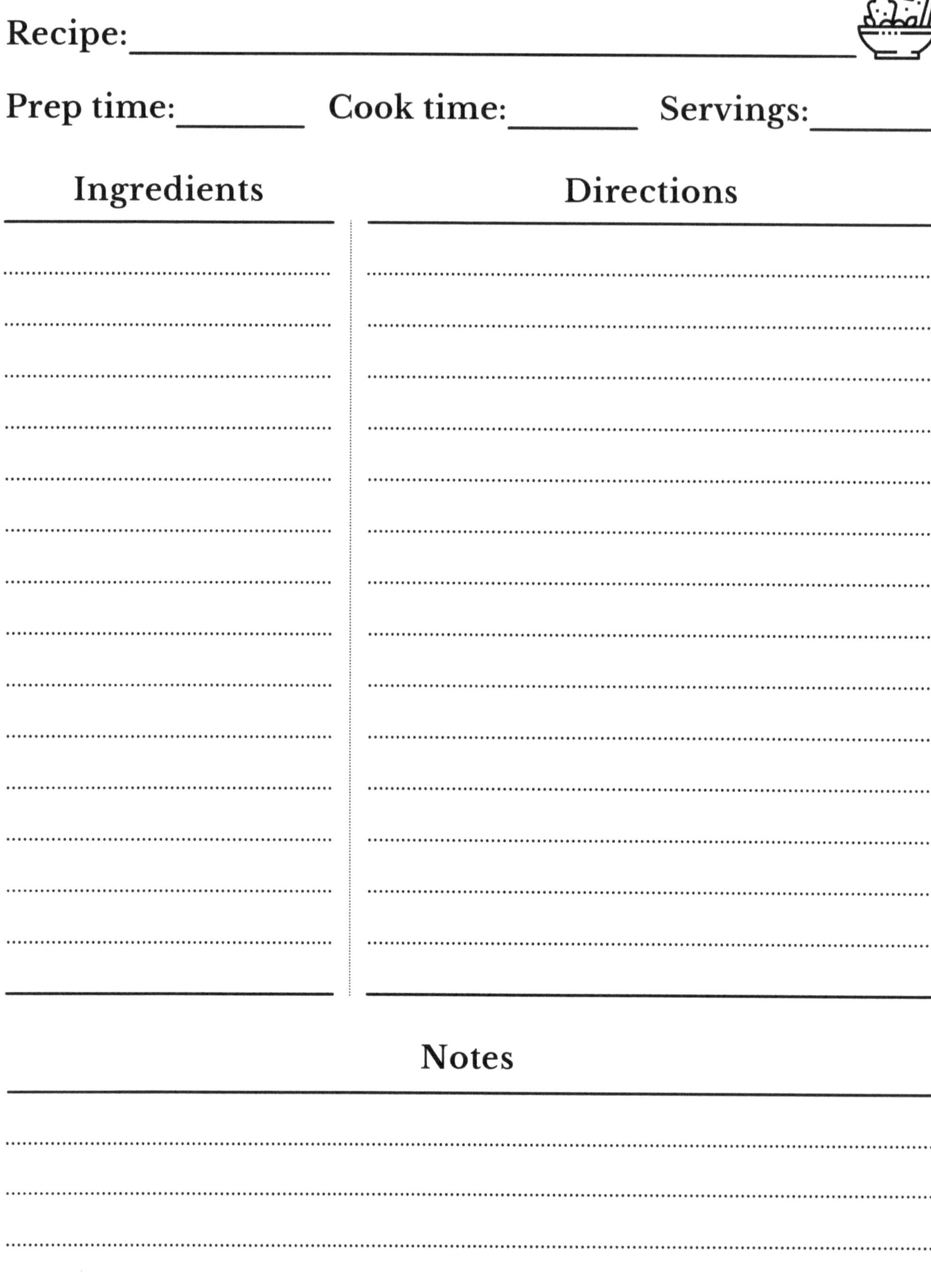

Recipe:____

Prep time:________   Cook time:________   Servings:________

Ingredients

Directions

Notes

Recipe: _______________________________ 

Prep time: _______ Cook time: _______ Servings: _______

Ingredients	Directions

Notes

Recipe:____ 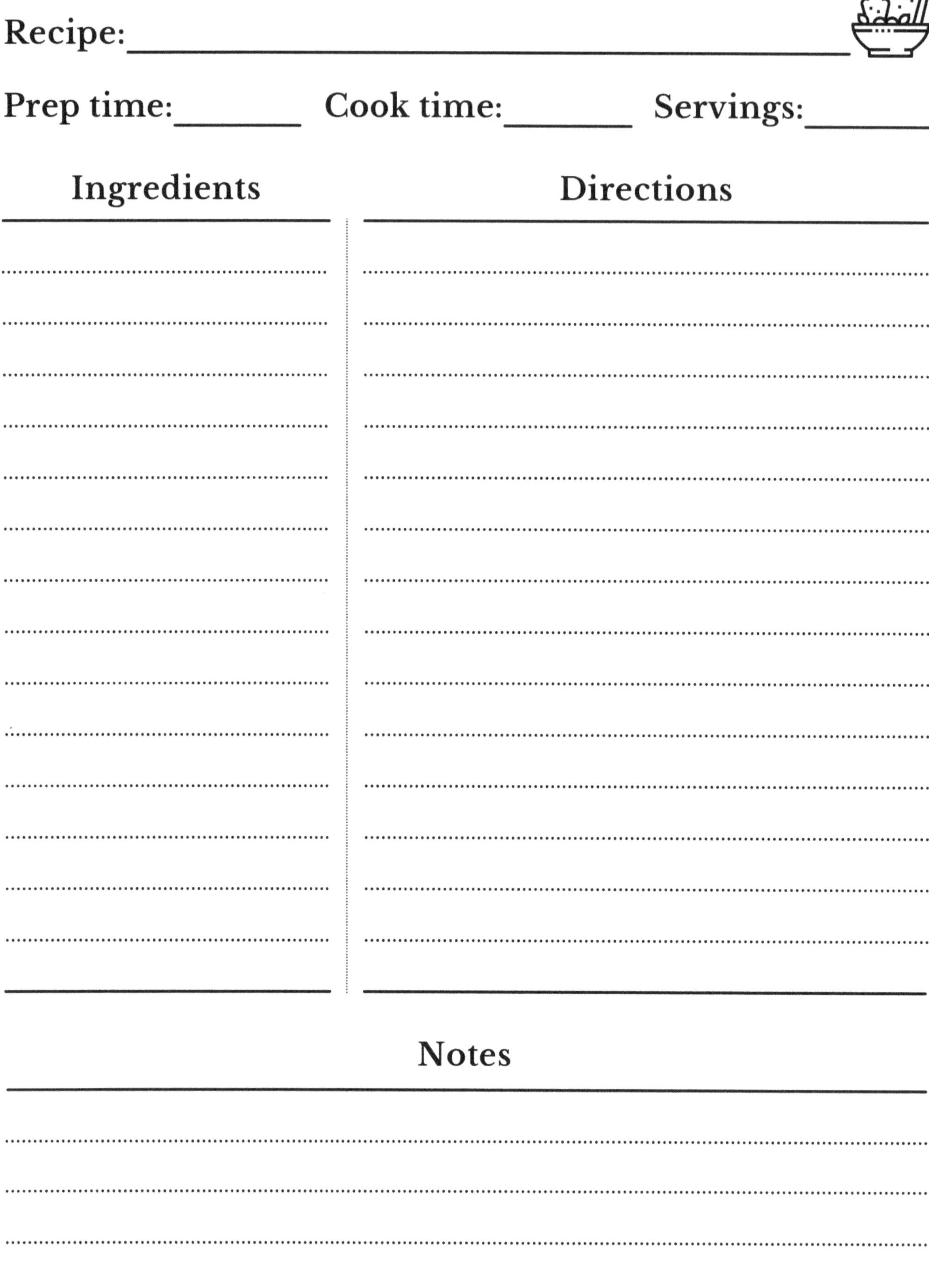

Prep time:________   Cook time:________   Servings:________

Ingredients

Directions

Notes

Recipe:_______________________________________ 

Prep time:_______   Cook time:_______   Servings:_______

Ingredients

Directions

Notes

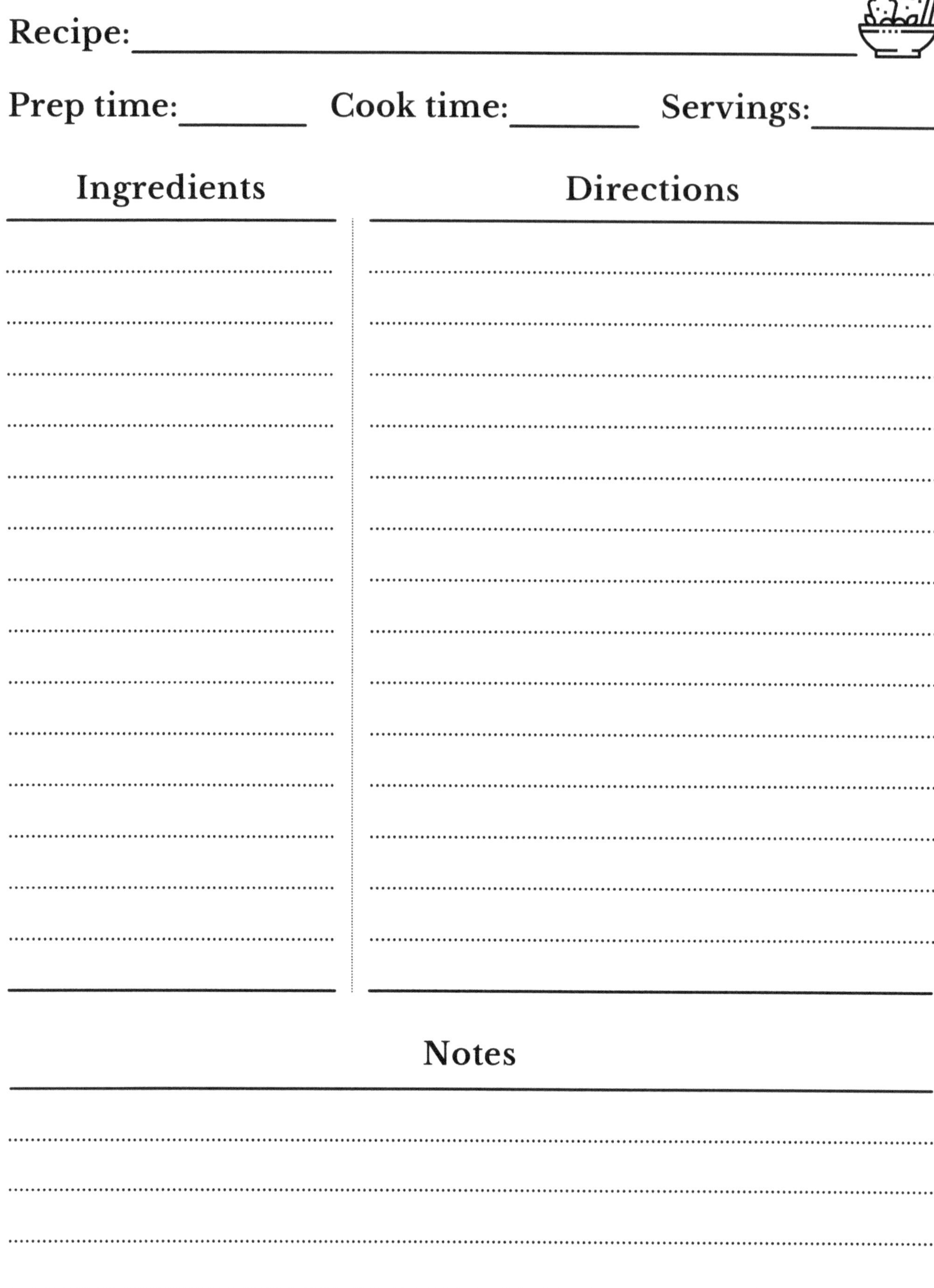

Recipe:_______________________________________

Prep time:________ Cook time:________ Servings:________

Ingredients

Directions

Notes

Recipe:_______________________________________ 

Prep time:_______   Cook time:_______   Servings:_______

Ingredients	Directions

Notes

Recipe:_______________________________________ 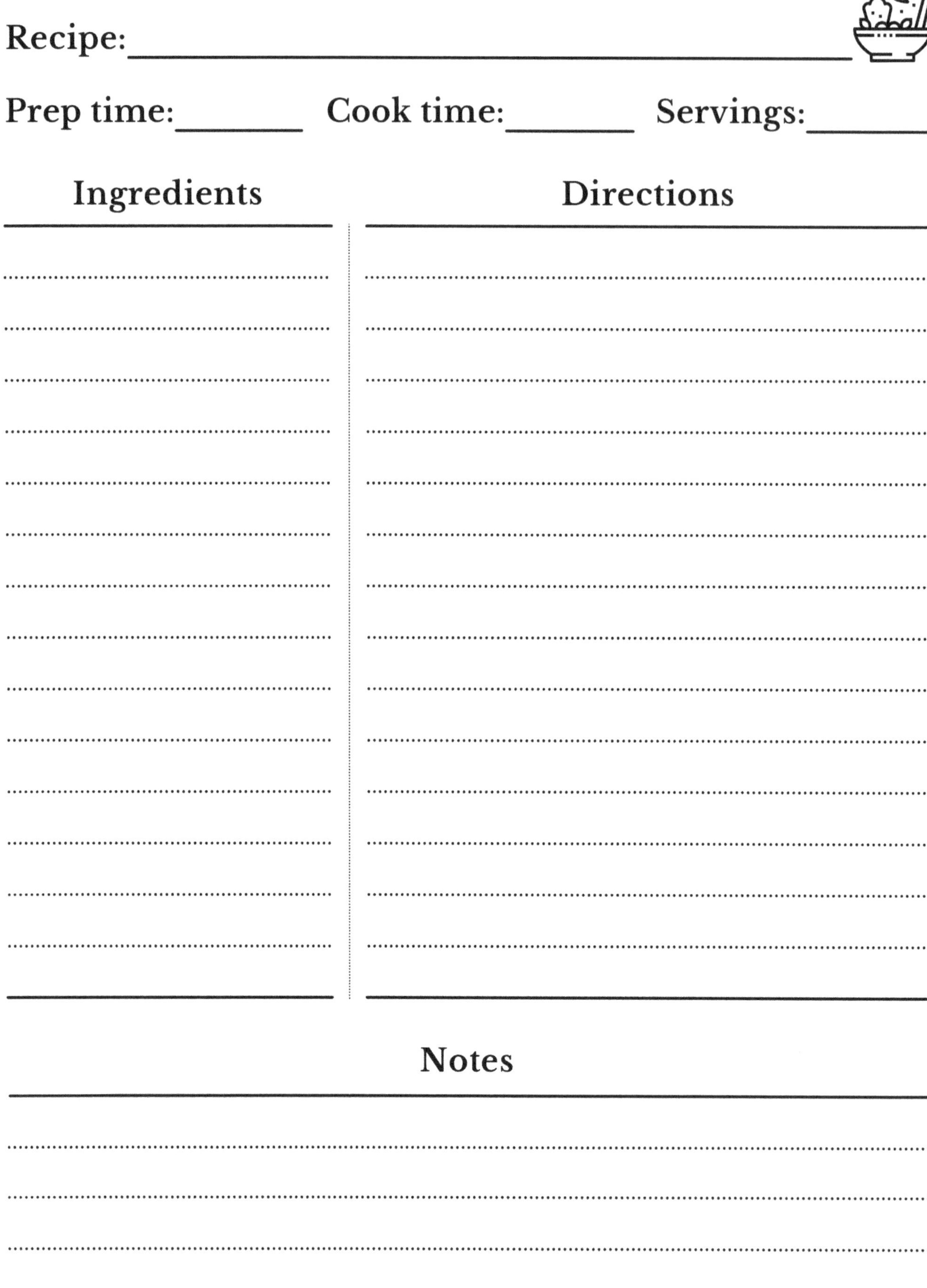

Prep time:________   Cook time:________   Servings:________

Ingredients
Directions

Notes

Recipe:____ 

Prep time:________ Cook time:________ Servings:________

Ingredients

Directions

Notes

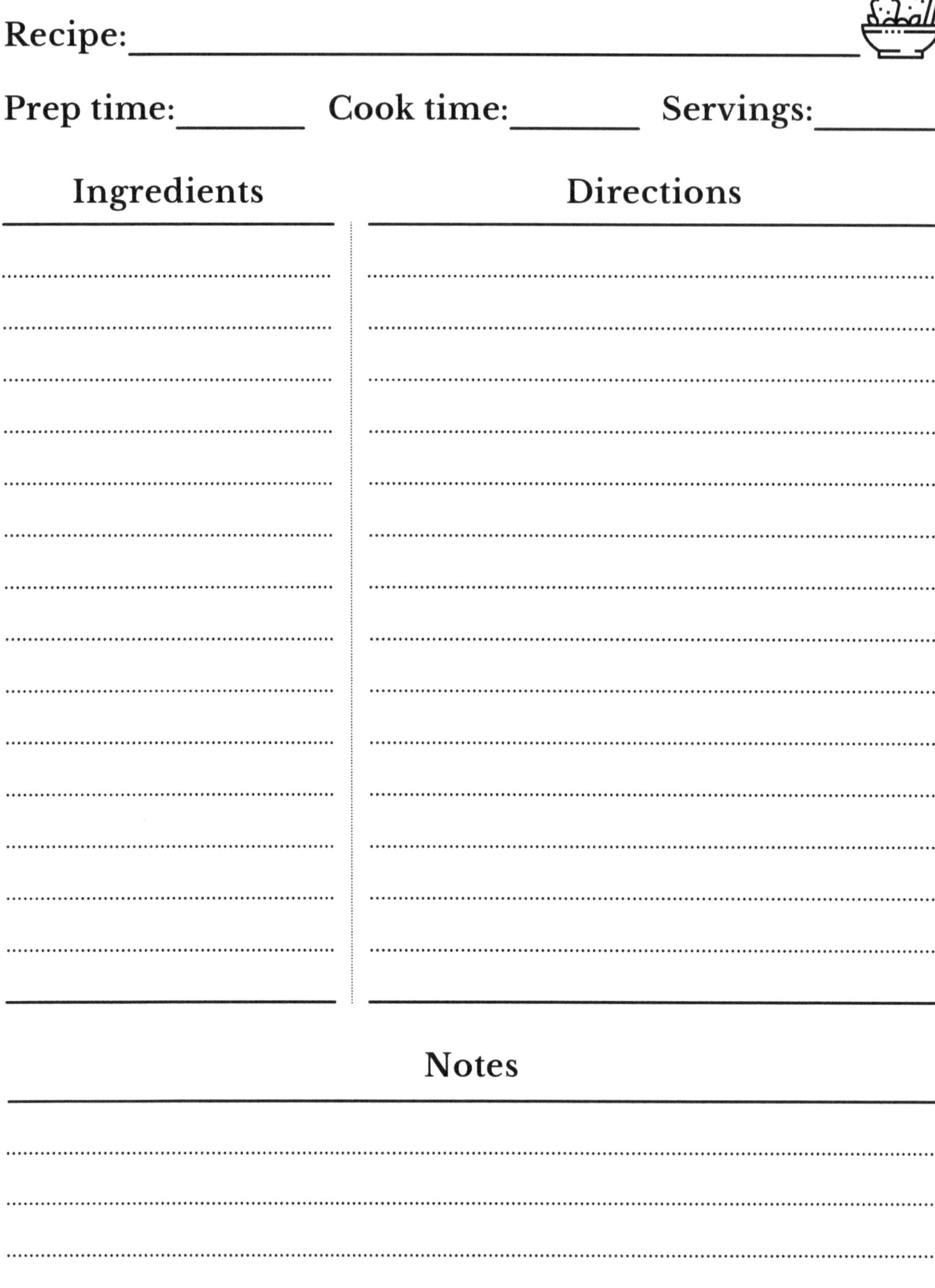

Recipe:____

Prep time:________ Cook time:________ Servings:________

Ingredients

Directions

Notes

Recipe:_______________________________________ 

Prep time:________   Cook time:________   Servings:________

Ingredients

Directions

Notes

Recipe:____

Prep time:________   Cook time:________   Servings:________

Ingredients	Directions

Notes

Recipe:_______________________________________ 

Prep time:________   Cook time:________   Servings:________

Ingredients

Directions

Notes

Recipe:____

Prep time:________ Cook time:________ Servings:________

Ingredients

Directions

Notes

Recipe: _______________________________ 

Prep time: _______   Cook time: _______   Servings: _______

Ingredients

Directions

Notes

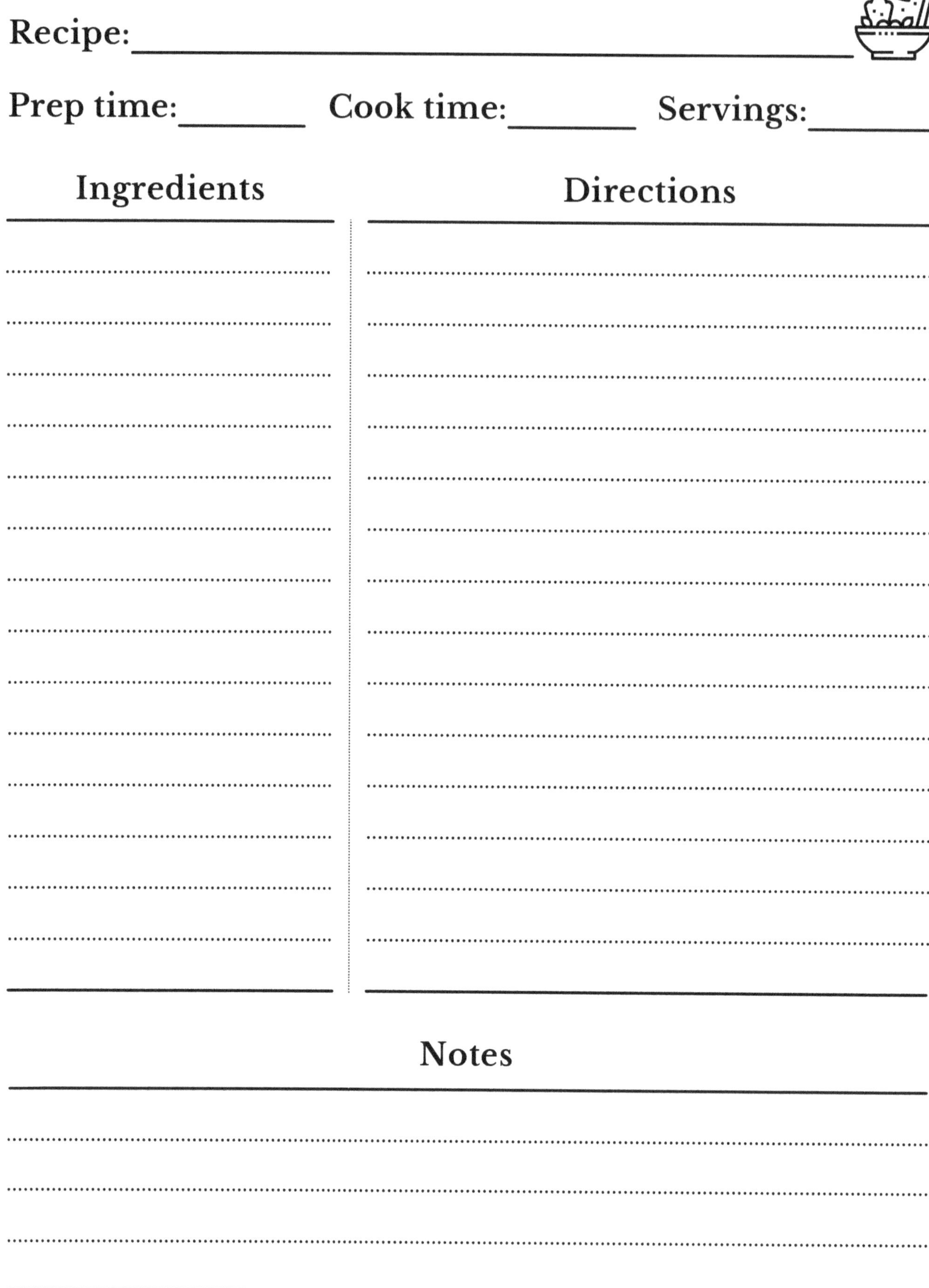

Recipe:____

Prep time:_______   Cook time:_______   Servings:_______

Ingredients

Directions

Notes

Recipe:

Prep time:________ **Cook time:**________ **Servings:**________

Ingredients

Directions

Notes

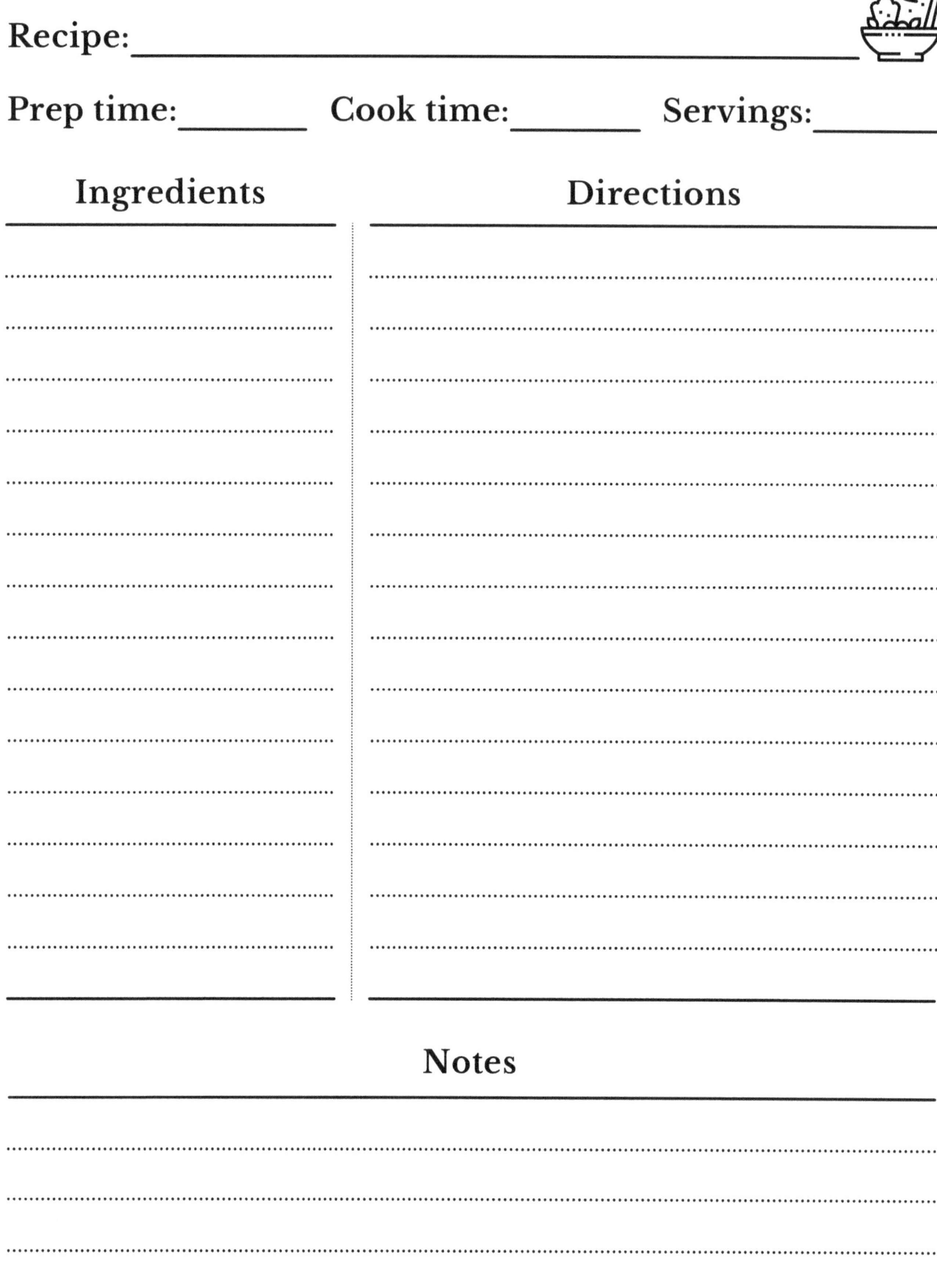

Recipe:____

Prep time:________   Cook time:________   Servings:________

Ingredients

Directions

Notes

Recipe:____ 

Prep time:________   Cook time:________   Servings:________

Ingredients

Directions

Notes

Recipe:_______________________________________

Prep time:________   Cook time:________   Servings:________

Ingredients

Directions

Notes

Recipe:____ 

Prep time:________   Cook time:________   Servings:________

Ingredients

Directions

Notes

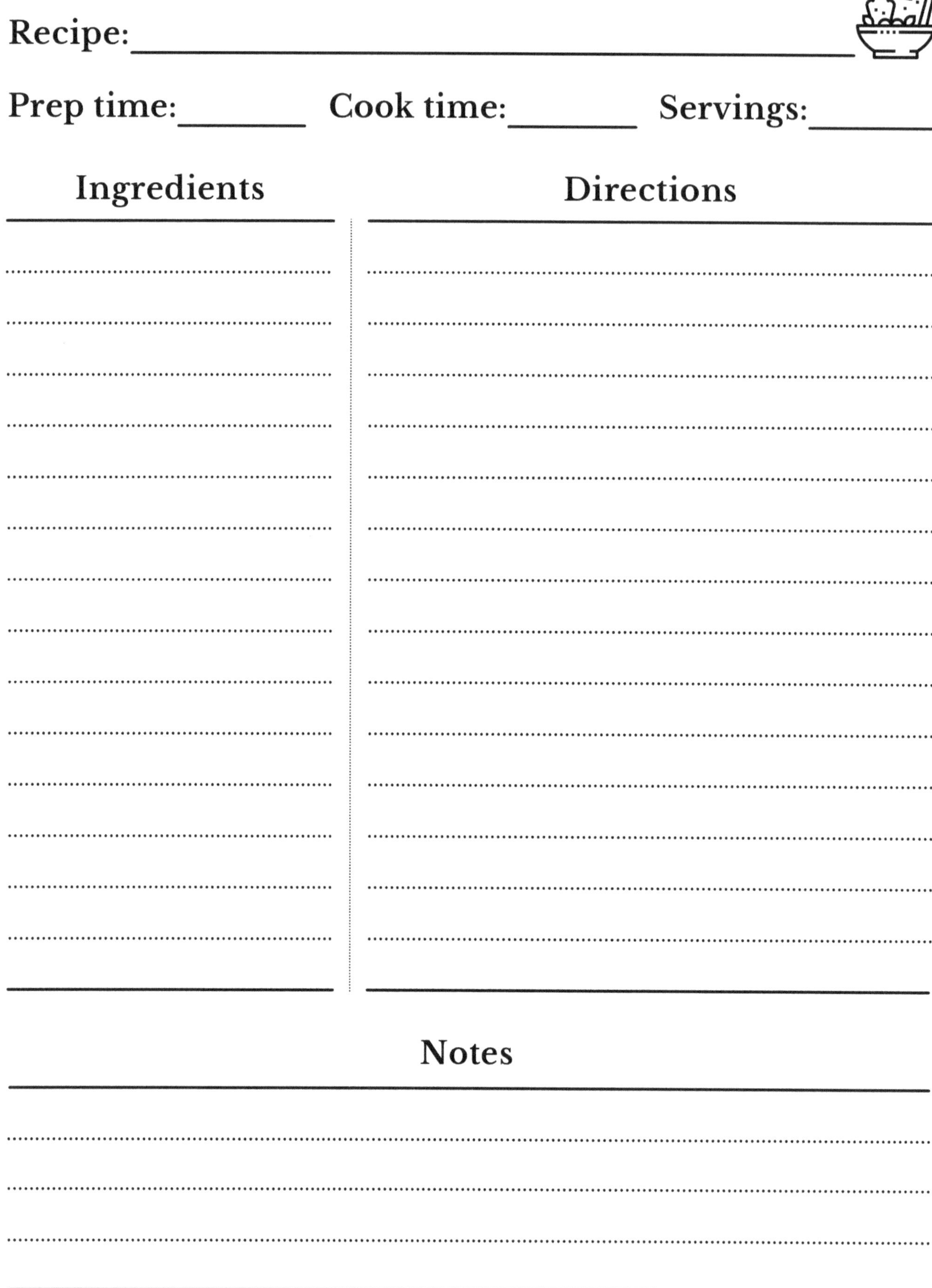

Recipe:____

Prep time:_________ **Cook time:**_________ **Servings:**_________

Ingredients   ## Directions

Notes

Recipe:____ 

Prep time:_______   Cook time:_______   Servings:_______

Ingredients | ## Directions

Notes

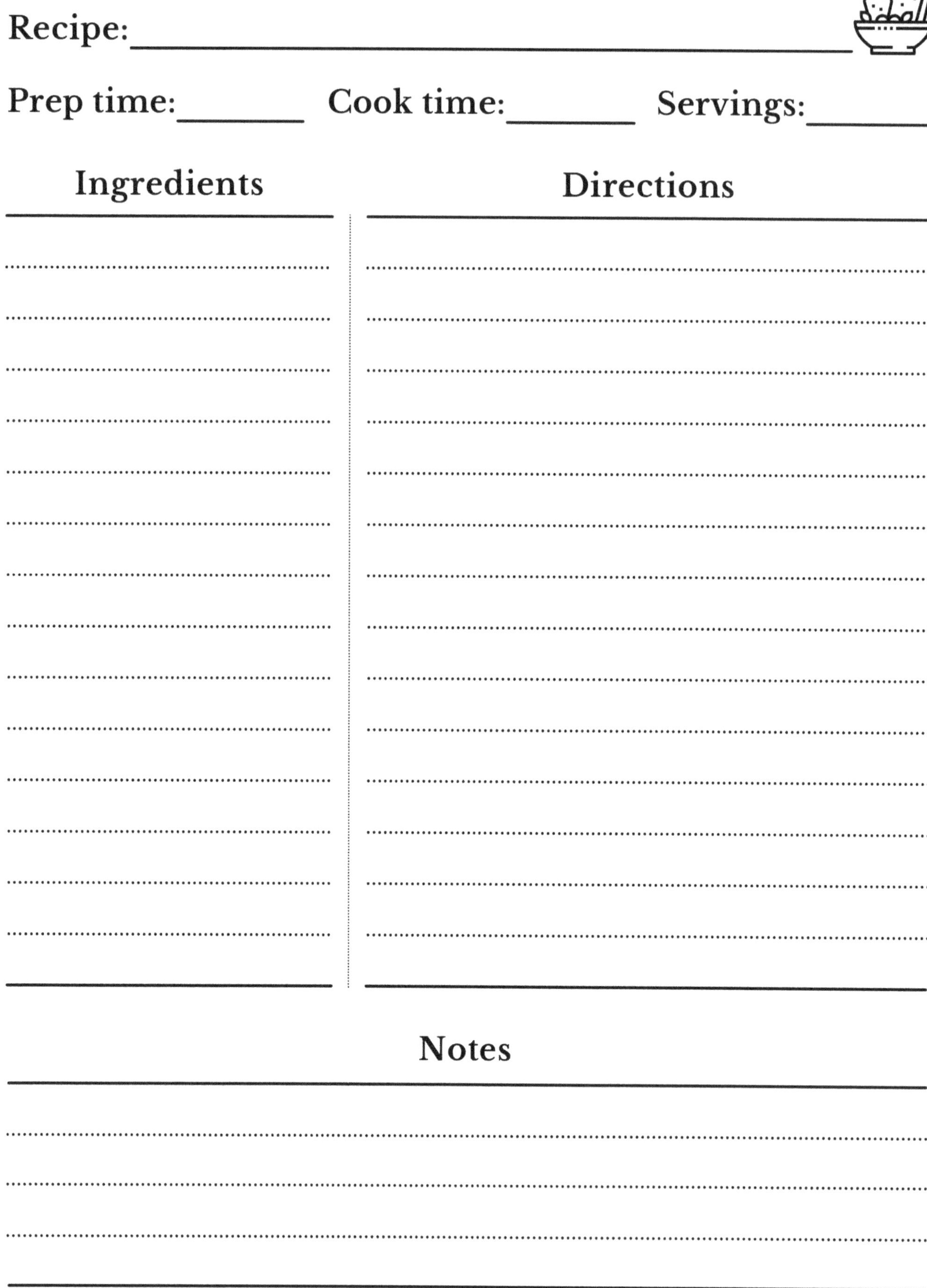

Recipe:

Prep time: **Cook time:** **Servings:**

Ingredients

Directions

Notes

Recipe:____ 

Prep time:________   Cook time:________   Servings:________

Ingredients	Directions

Notes

Recipe:____

Prep time:_________ Cook time:_________ Servings:_________

Ingredients

Directions

Notes

Recipe:_______________________________ 

Prep time:_______ **Cook time:**_______ **Servings:**_______

Ingredients

Directions

Notes

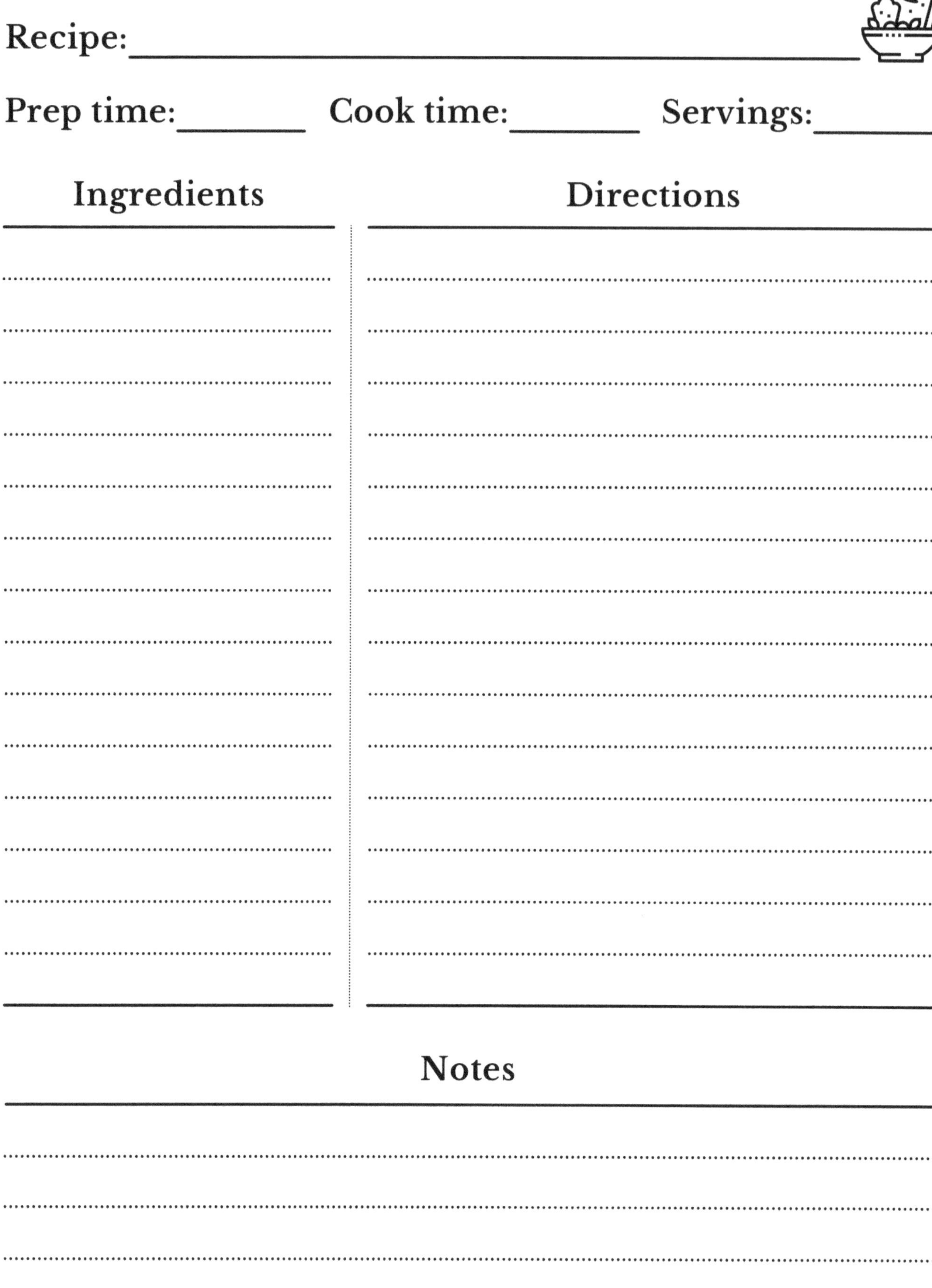

Recipe:____

Prep time:________   Cook time:________   Servings:________

Ingredients

Directions

Notes

Recipe:___________________________________ 

Prep time:_______   Cook time:_______   Servings:_______

Ingredients

Directions

Notes

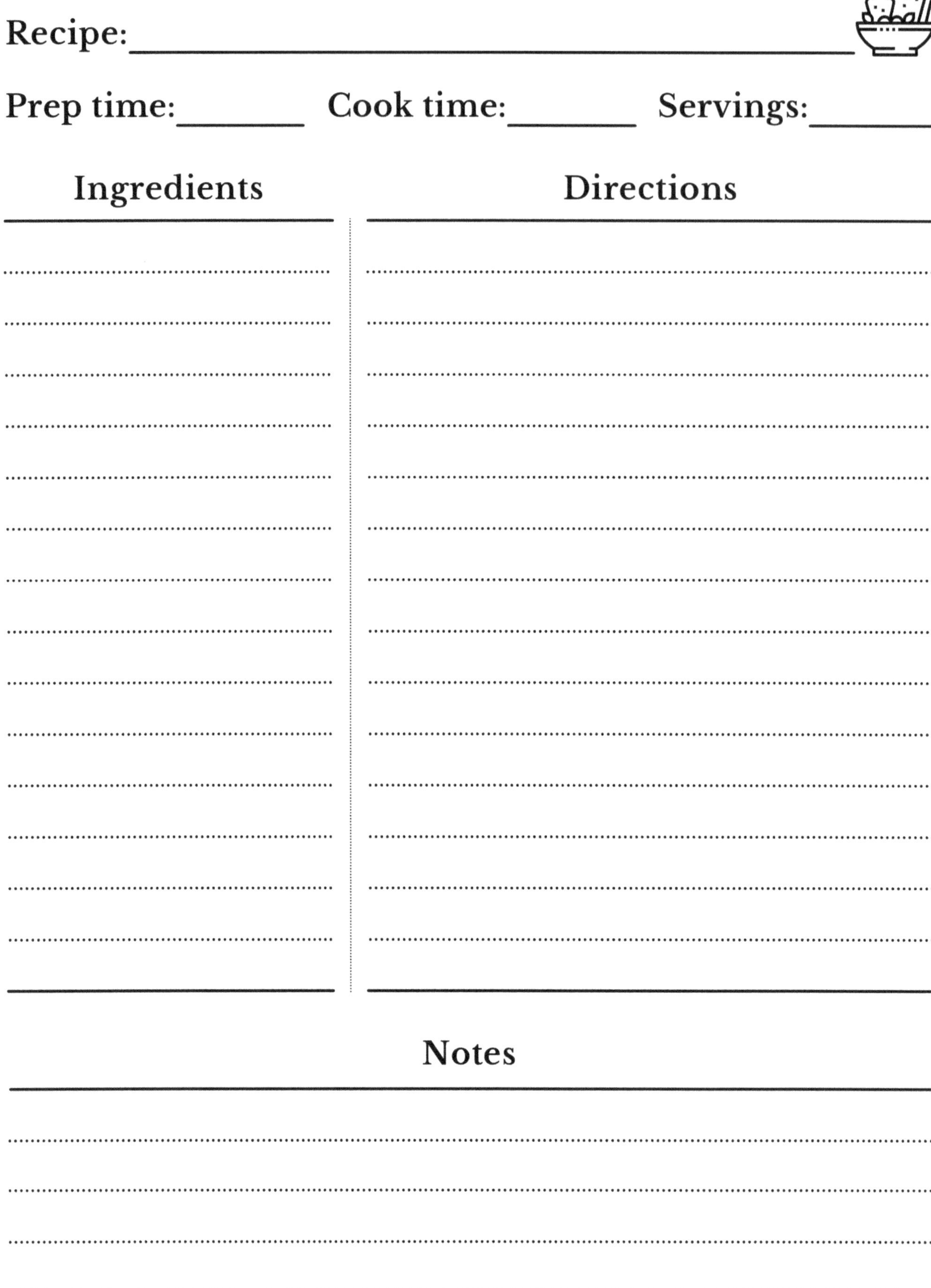

Recipe:____

Prep time:________ Cook time:________ Servings:________

Ingredients

Directions

Notes

Recipe:_______________________________________ 

Prep time:_______   Cook time:_______   Servings:_______

Ingredients

Directions

Notes

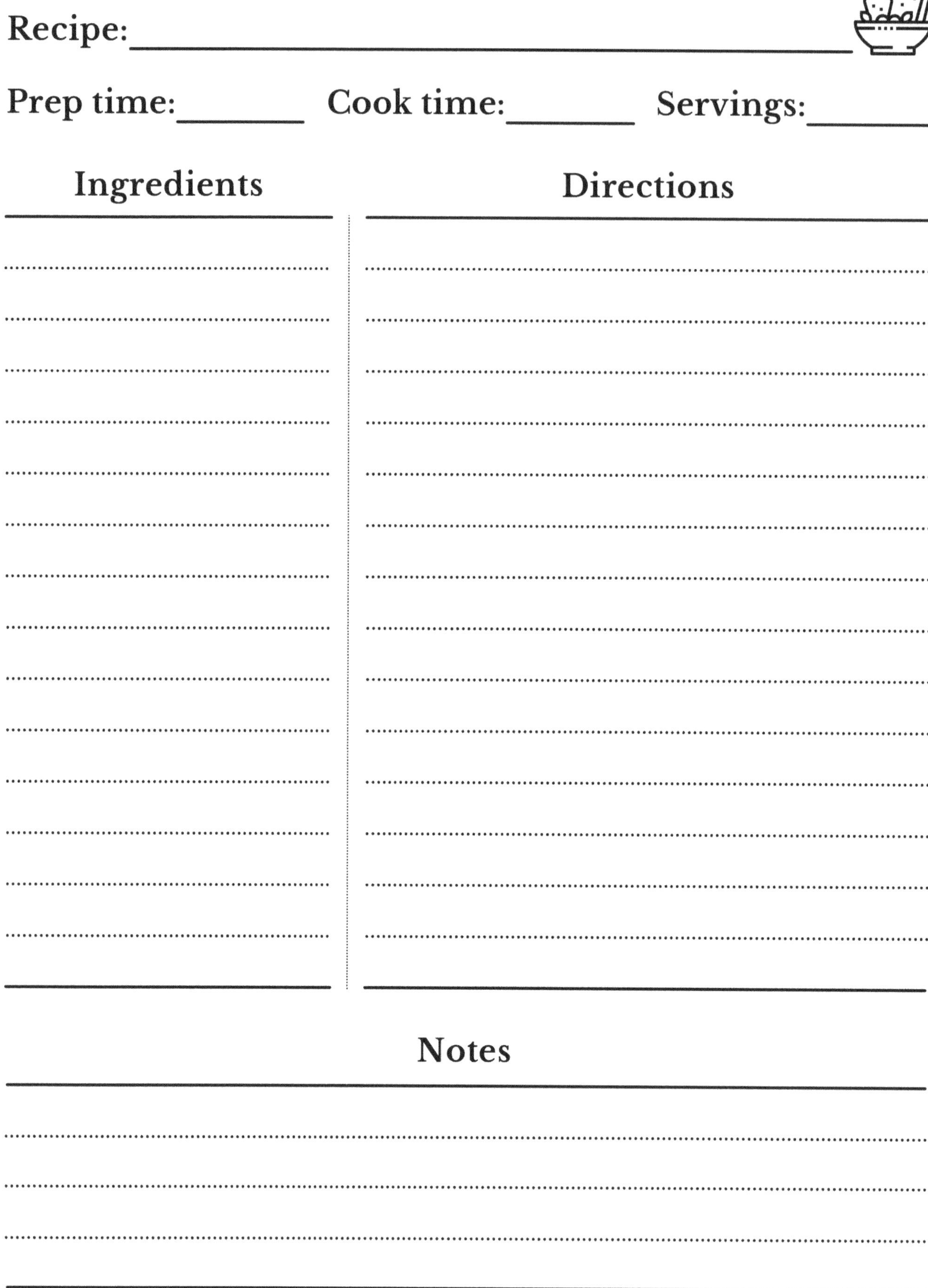

Recipe:____

Prep time:________   Cook time:________   Servings:________

Ingredients

Directions

Notes

Recipe:____ 

Prep time:________   Cook time:________   Servings:________

Ingredients

Directions

Notes

Recipe:

Prep time: ______ Cook time: ______ Servings: ______

Ingredients

Directions

Notes

Recipe:___________________________________

Prep time:_______   Cook time:_______   Servings:_______

Ingredients

....
....
....
....
....
....
....
....
....
....
....
....

Directions

....
....
....
....
....
....
....
....
....
....
....
....
....
....
....

Notes

....
....
....

Recipe:____

Prep time:_________ Cook time:_________ Servings:_________

| Ingredients | Directions |

Notes

Recipe: _______________________________ 

Prep time: _______   Cook time: _______   Servings: _______

Ingredients

Directions

Notes

Recipe:____

Prep time:________   Cook time:________   Servings:________

Ingredients

Directions

Notes

Recipe:

Prep time:_______ **Cook time:**_______ **Servings:**_______

Ingredients | Directions

Notes

Recipe:____

Prep time:________   Cook time:________   Servings:________

Ingredients

Directions

Notes

Recipe:

Prep time:_______   Cook time:_______   Servings:_______

Ingredients

Directions

Notes

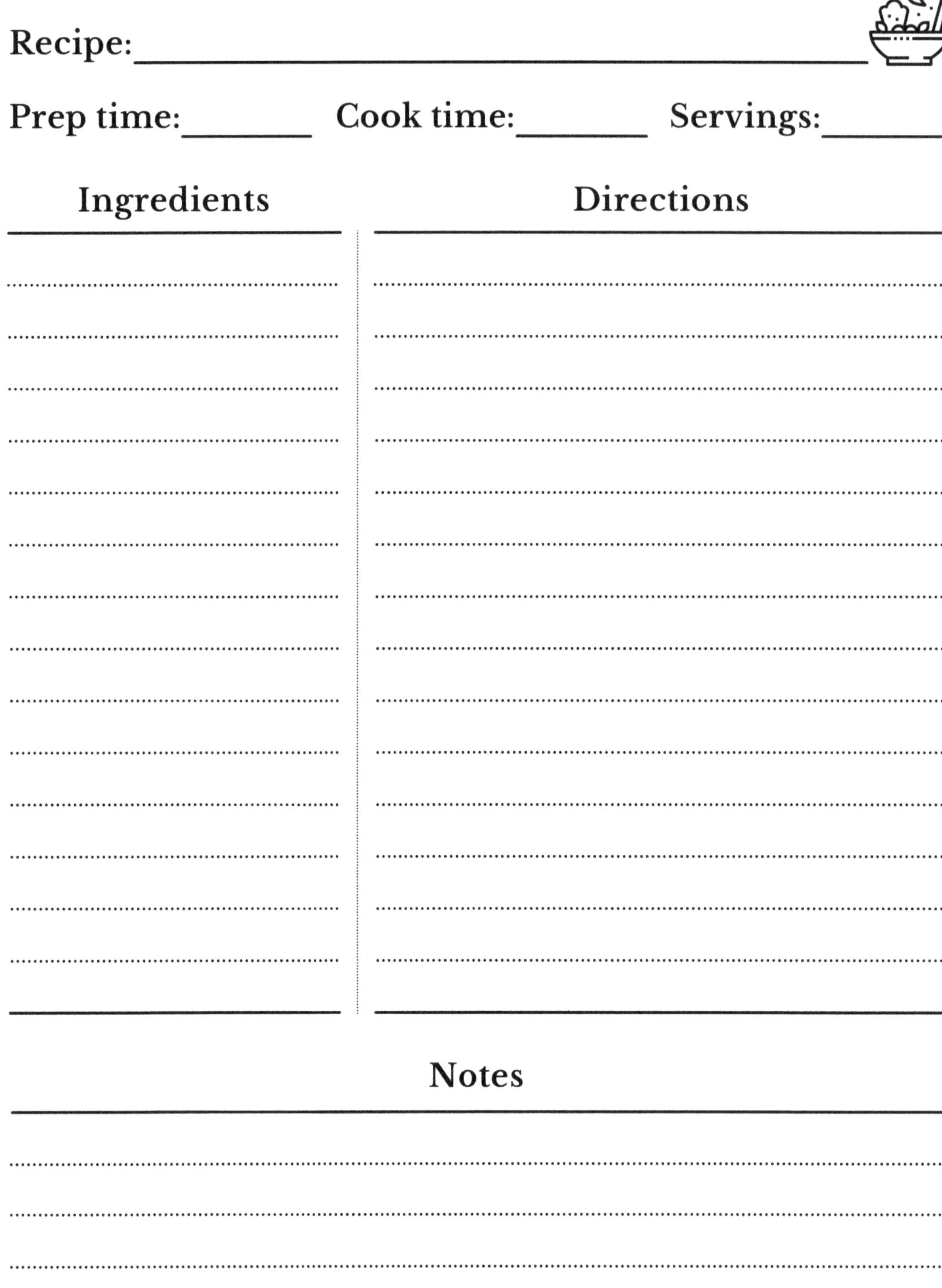

Recipe:

Prep time: ________ **Cook time:** ________ **Servings:** ________

Ingredients

Directions

Notes